A Sabbath Among the Ruins

A Sabbath Among the Ruins

Deena Metzger

PARALLAX PRESS
BERKELEY, CALIFORNIA

Acknowledgments

Invocation L.A.
The Streets Inside: Ten Los Angeles Poets
Gramercy Review
The Dolphin's Arc, Poems of Endangered Creatures
of the Sea
Poetry/LA
The San Fernando Valley: Past and Present
Changing Landscapes
Word of Mouth, 1
Word of Mouth, 2
New Letters
Bachy
Electrum
The Listening Life
The Brooklyn College Alumni Literary Review
Zero
Pleasures: Women Write Erotica
Erotic By Nature
Worlds of Prayer

Cover and book design by Lawrence Watson
Front cover drawing by Ikazo
Back cover photograph by Hella Hammid
Copyright © 1992 by Deena Metzger
All rights reserved
Printed in the U.S.A.
ISBN 0-938077-53-8

A portion of the proceeds from the sale of
A Sabbath Among the Ruins will go to the
Buddhist Peace Fellowship.

PARALLAX PRESS
P.O. Box 7355, Berkeley, California 94707

For Michael, my love,
and for all the endangered creatures.

Contents

WALKING WITH NERUDA

Preface

These poems were written over many years. They emerge from the ruins in which we are living, from my despair of finding a Sabbath, from my persistent search for it, and from the unexpected discovery that the Sabbath exists even in the midst of devastation.

This is the Sabbath: a little rain in the midst of drought, vision in the very moment of understanding nothing, a flash of beauty in a broken bowl, and the miraculous, insistent vitality of the body and the heart.

I could have eliminated the earlier poems, the poems of grief and injury, the poems of the broken heart, but how then, would we recognize the Sabbath, and all it endures in order to shine?

In gratitude, then, for the gift of the seventh day,

Deena Metzger
Topanga Canyon
Santa Monica Mountains, 1992

Invocation

Some of us have spent our lifetimes
searching our bodies
for the letters of flame,
when they arise
some of us burn
and some of us set fires.

Forgetting the Light

Driving bougainvillaea to the summit like sheep, like a herd of singing goats, like a grove of trees, into the mountains where the heart, if allowed, may spring open like a fountain of bees.

I can look at the land and forget. It disappears from my heart without warning and where it was, a scar.

Melons break apart in the sweet dark like great moons overflowing the banisters of night. The fruits of knowledge, sticky on the fingers, tasted and despised.

We forget everything. The alphabet of stars, an impenetrable foreign script eternally incomprehensible in the moment of turning aside, of washing the hands. Yet everything known by the yucca in the heat of day. Blossoms, cool as white horses, rising in a scented plume to the sundial of light.

"Why are you here?" they ask, beckoning to the shadows we cast, opening their mouths, shy.

Ignorance, turning away, the undertow, pulls us through the mud. Nothing in the word. Nothing before the word. Nothing under it and afterwards and beyond. And the flank of the sea, ready, shuddering, waiting to be known.

Pine tumbling toward the stream in the pulse of deer, in the rain of moose, in the gasp of stone. A blue birth in the eye of corn. A nest of feathers and wind. Stamens afire. Lizards uncircumcised and wanton in their faith. And the night flowers taking the watch of the morning birds.

"Why are you here?" they ask. "And why are you afraid?"

"I remember," I say. "I remember," I say. In that instant the sun, that great egg, cracks in a smithy of fire.

"Then please, don't speak," they say. "Then please don't speak of it. Please don't speak anymore," they say.

In the silence, then, in the silence, then, everything of earth and everything of water, everything of air, and everything of fire, rushing with so much stillness, forward and forever, into the very first breath.

M a g u e y

For Michael

Like the zen master,
you came with the sword.

The gentle woman who taught me, said
"The rose and the thorn."
You want to catch in my flesh.

I watch the century plant
shoot a green staff into the air.

I tell you how the stamens hook
out of the stalk, they will...

'Flower,' you say,
wanting the yellow rain,

pulque, mescal, tequilla
out of the green spiny leaves.

Walking to the olive tree,
thistles catch in my clothes,
burrs in my hands and feet,

everything asking to be carried.
Why do you weep in rage,
when I cry out?

Even the buddha wolf knows the spike,
carries seeds from one place to another;
they grasp at him.

The crown of thorns:
the life holding on.

The Huichols say, "In this life
no one goes lacking
for something with which to get stuck in the eye."

In the desert
we become tenacious.

How did we say it when I was a kid?
"I'm hooked."

The day you visit:
Maguey—a green maypole
out of a rosette of razors

speeds past my window—
twelve feet in a week
—to dissolve in sperm milk of yellow flowers.

Still, we cannot pretend
it is easy.

Across the barbed wire, the bull takes my hand. It is
lost in his mouth, deeper, softer, warmer than I dare
think. This is what it must be to sink into a large
woman, to submit to her ample thighs. I am aware of
boundaries, his teeth, used to grass, will not close on
me, he wants the salt, wants me to sweat for him.

I have had to come east to learn this animal, a real
not mythic beast, attended by dozens of heifers, who
seeks me out under the horned, full moon. My hands,
stained with mulberries, come clean on that great
tongue slapping between my fingers, his tail flits
across his back, his silken tassel quivers.

I have dreamed this animal but not his gentleness,
not that I would herd with him, not that I would
wish him to nudge my flanks, his skin slouched over
bones, a tent of a beast, not that he would drive me
forward

        head down
            hungry
                through the
                    night fields.

"I have heard it before," Barbara says, disappointed that after twenty years she should be picking up a poem to find the same dilemma unsolved. The moon is milky. We walk out of the house to say good-bye. "We take lovers," I tell her, "to remember the sky." She is not pleased that after twenty years, I have not learned there is something fresher in the wind. Above us the invaded and defeated moon glows with that eerie light, the white heat of its pulse eats against my skin and pulls on the white geyser in the body. "It's the same milk cry," I say. "You've said that before," she says, "and the theme of milk boiling in you has been there for twenty years." We've talked about this liquid which is the oil of us, the riches in us, but though my fingers reach to it, I have not gotten closer. What it is the fingers strive to clutch remains stubbornly ungraspable beneath the skin.

"I have heard this before," Barbara says, and yet I am not through with it this evening of the milky sky when the white haze reminds me that tomorrow, the miracle, obvious and constant as the morning paper, will still elude me as I squint to read the headlines, taking in the airplane crashes, fires, shooting deaths and oil spills; and the men upon the moon no nearer to the white oil than I am.

In the morning, I will need to know again how it is the world turns and remains on the same point, the principles of rotation and revolution which I remember from high school science, and that the moon turns twice also but along an egg following the sun. We stand on point like a dancer lost in the moment, the little dolls on Broadway that sailors buy, the music box devoted to the perpetual ballerina, if there are still sailors like the ones I found on the subway and brought home. Or are they now the adventurers who sweep in from the white Alaska pipeline, thin, acned, scared and full of small bills and coins in their pockets, looking to sleep on water beds and rock with the lunar tide or to bend in the broken curve of old mattresses after being fed on the same sandwiches of rye bread and leftover roast? And what do they have to do with milk, those who pass the black tar across the tundra, casting the same shadows on the snow that the man casts who steps with his boots upon the moon.

Twenty-five years after the sailors, there is the same ache and the same illusive sweat upon the skin, the same nerves, the same certainty in my body that there is something to be known which I have not come to know. I remember the sailor who climbed into my car at a red light, pressing a knife to my ribs in the daytime when the moon hid long enough for me to drive into a gas station—SUNOCO—and he got out casually grinning moonily, "Thanks for the ride, baby." Something to be gotten at which remains elusive as those sailors whose names I don't remember, coming from the Broadway dark into my house to be fed bread cut with a butcher knife.

To be adolescent again, reduced in my womanhood to the same awkward teenager as ignorant as my own small sons and continuing to poke in a brazen manner, index finger, thumb, blade, into the places which yield. And coming to the smell of it, more odor than the aftertaste of goat in the milk, and a new love growing in me swelling crescents, fourteen days to turn and fourteen days back. And it's time to milk the cows again, they bleat with the fullness in their udders, but the city girl can't pull it out fast enough. She doesn't have the muscle or the rhythm to milk the teats dry, and there's something in the formula of milk she doesn't understand as she sits there talking to the cows, listening to their incomprehensible mooing. It's in your body and in mine, something I haven't found yet and no one seems to know or care though some advise moon ships and rocket probes to find new images, but this sticks like an old skin of milk.

"Why is it," she asks, "it is with a man that you look at the moon?" I repeat, "It is why we take lovers." A friend said we could control our bodies by sleeping in an absolutely dark room, black silk sheets over the windows. Open the window once during the month and turn the skin to the moonlight and the egg will push out toward it and wait its three days, waxing and waning, before it drops away. In the night of the moonlight, you must not sleep with a man unless you want a child.

So the old images persist as the moon reappears. Neither the twenty years of poems nor the landing ships and scientific instruments from Texas have exhausted this old obsession or revealed anything, but that something lies beneath the surfaces we raze with metal scoops to find metals or some white oil to keep the heat burning. The blunt miracle of cheese persisting while we sit around the pool with our chests naked to the sun, the ordinary genitals turning slightly pink. Despite our casual demeanor, I do not tell you about the sailors I brought home or the soldiers that I danced with in army camps, because, as I said then, "They are lonely and there is no war on." Was it because they didn't speak any language I knew that we danced and looked up at the moon and the man in it and said good-bye with sweaty palms and bellies full of legal moonshine. And I wonder about the men who go off to build the pipelines in Alaska and attack caribou which graze upon the moon. And what does the astronaut launched in Florida and controlled in Texas think as his space ship scratches the moon dust and what does he learn with his crude metallic instruments which probe the dark side?

And I confess a turning point: In the park learning the Tai Chi forms which are the black and white crescents of the moon, the Guernsey cow, I found another soldier who asked if he could learn the rhythms too. "I am a mercenary," he said, "and round in my motions." I didn't take out my little Swiss army knife and stab delicate half circles between his ribs. I didn't ask him whom he killed, which of my sisters or brothers he had dropped fire on, which of the people the sun burns dark, he had darkened further, but said he could learn the moon dance, thinking it might burn into him, white as napalm, as he had burned death into others and that then the larger blade in his hand might drop from it.

Something from the dark teases me as you walk toward me from a nightmare the first night we spend together, the moon coming over our bodies and the trees playing animal shapes against the light. You wake afraid that I will tear your common secret from you without knowing that it has been twenty-seven years I have been looking for it, and it still waves at me like a sailor saying he is going back to the ship when I know the man entering the subway is only retreating to Broadway and to the little dolls which twirl, to the music boxes, the post cards, the women who know how to wear black stockings and white shoes, and to the boys whose pants are even tighter than mine across the ass. I also learned the fashion of that street, wore boots with little moon shaped heels, sharp as scimitars, and leather belts tight about my waist, and pushed up my breasts over crescents of wire so that they looked like plump moons.

But with all the instruments created for exploration, something eludes me, and maybe it is because in the last instant after the sheets open to the moonlight, I don't dare be anything but polite. Lying down, clean and ready for the body which approaches me with familiar passion, knowing each time there is something I don't dare, ignorant of how to dare it.

Knowing now that the moon has no voices, that it is quieter than I thought and not to be gotten at with a knife as I had imagined, fantasizing, and not daring, the switchblade in my own hand, used against my own self, ripping my own body open so someone can enter. "I've heard this before," Barbara says. "Yes," I answer, "but this time it's different; see where we are in the orbit."

Do you remember, Barbara, the man in New York who passed us wearing a little silver razor blade about his neck? Later you learned it was for cocaine, white moon powder, but I thought it was only for violence and still believe I'm right. Remember the little pocket knives flicked into the dirt as we played marbles, trading hard swirling moons and carrying them home clicking, blue white and moonstone against the steel blades and coming in thirsty for a cold glass of milk? "I've heard all this before," Barbara repeats, but listens while I go off looking, because I can hear, without seeing, the voices in the bushes teasing, "You're hot; you're cold." like the two sides of the moon.

I remember that yesterday we drove across the city and I saw the moon red and fat and close as a belly and I said, "Look, look, at the moon." But there was something in the way of your seeing it. The moon was playing hide and seek with us behind buildings and I said, "Let's go to the top of the hill so you can see it," and agreeing you drove straight on saying you had seen the moon before. And suddenly it didn't matter, we had both seen the moon before and it would return faithful to its fourteen days of coming and going.

"I want to understand the body." "You always do," she says, "when you're in love. You think the body can catch something and hold it like it catches a child." The moon is quiet.

There is no air. You can not talk there. When we get there it's hot or cold, and the light or dark we chase hovers through the dust we kick up with our big metal feet. We are mute and dumb there and look aside while the common secret balances just out of reach. And having used a knife before, I turn aside from it without scorn for those who wield it, knowing what desperation brings them to cut, stab, slash, a knife going into the broken mattress looking for coins and green bills, while the bird feathers fly in a white haze about the room. It isn't there. It isn't with a knife we find it, but there is a common secret just beyond the sperm and orgasm, or just before it, a simple coupling like the light of the sun upon the moon. I can't ignore the man in the moon or the shadow of black and white.

The moon never stops turning, and we turn with it, a dancer on point, we travel that ellipse around the sun and the first hint of the moon, like a little trickle of white thin milk, slips across the sky as we sit under an apricot tree. You cut a fruit into half circles and there's the bleat of the goat around us, only it is just a dog barking, and the next door neighbors making love in front of the blue glow of the television set, and while there is still something I want to know, it's fading as the sun and moon angle from each other.

And I may have to wait another month to know the common secret, to end the mystery once and for all by entering it through the early dark places, the ordinary doorways, where the sailors disappear. Or by standing silently under the constant moon which sees the dark earth coming and knows what turns in that turning.

S pirit wraps itself about a mote of dust, a speck of green in the endless sky, then falls wet and dark into the rivers and the hungry clay. So it repeats itself— not history, but creation.

In the beginning was fire and the rain came later. Rain came out of the fire from the very breast of light. Then the light continued, falling, wrapping itself about the leaves, gleaming on the dark feathers, glittering in the fur. And the rain followed it to make a bed for everything which burns.

She had decided to love us. She came out of the night and tempered the starry fire in her lap of water. She rained down milk and honey, a carnival of bees amidst the lowing of the cattle.

The way the clouds hold the light, shimmer after the lightning has struck, the way fog glows when it holds the moon, is the way the water held us after the fire fall.

The love of water for the fire. The desire of spirit for the hands of rain. And the flame, which loses itself in love, is alive everywhere, even in the burning fish which shine in the nether regions of the sea.

To hold the flame. To sustain the flame against the wind and all the elements. To preserve the flame always in water—this is the task.

It had all been fire to begin with. All fire from beginning to end until She sent rain into the body of stars. But when we arose in our watery grief, we were afraid of burning and made a covenant with the dark. Then fear brought us down through an eon of water and a torrent of salt onto a promontory of rock.

And so the darkness came and the fire was extinguished. Without that fire, the rivers reversed themselves, rose up blind to the sky, streaking like frozen comets, sunward. And the oceans rose too, raining down elsewhere, far from the green place, and the earth remained without fire and without rain. What we have left to us, then, is the empty bed of drought, is the death rattle of leaves, is the parched tongue, is the mote of dust, an unraveling swirl of dust whirling about itself.

So now you, you, who were afraid, call the fire down for the laying on of hands onto the body earth. Now, you, call the burning water down for the nest of green. Now, you, begin again, and open yourself to blaze and to drown in the last possible storm of light.

Whoever is willing to speak, take in the rain which burns the tongue and set out. Set out, burning and wet and alone, for the groves of prayer, so the great trees may glisten again in the rain of fire you dare—for Her—knowing we will survive.

Endangered Species

For Victor

If it were only a question of whales, but it isn't. If it were only a matter of finding one creature we wanted to save. If we could choose one and remain with it, a faithful mate through our lifetime, or even through centuries. If we were afflicted with only a single obsession, if we could call ourselves Ahab, or Joan, intent upon a single battle, a single enemy, if it were only a matter of passion, a silver image about our necks, a solitary obsession, a personal truth, a clear and simple vengeance.

If it were only a matter of a single commitment, if the passion did not wear thin, if it were not discarded, if it did not slide from us as if the weight had gone out from us, the shoulders too thin, the hips inadequate for that garment. If it were only a matter of a single hate, a single general, a single pain, we took and wore, we could keep it in repair, could nurture it, our beloved enemy.

If it were only a question of whales, of one, but it isn't. If there weren't a thousand calling us. If when I saw you, I saw only a dolphin, let us say, and you saw only a lonely woman, or madness. Only one, or another, endangered species. If it were only one creature in danger of extinction you carried, if we were not called to by a thousand voices, if my arms were not so full, if your arms were not so full, then, it is possible, we could embrace.

But we stand at arm's length. Such fidelity as I crave, isn't possible. One creature slips from our arms and another enters like so many lovers. We can not hold on to each other. In the midst of the calling, we are more faithful to pain than the creatures who enter our bodies. The wars continue. More dolphins churn in the net. The deaths of the dark skinned peoples increase. The air is difficult to breathe. I find our deaths translated into a thousand screeches.

My arms are heavy. I do not know how much more I can carry, but the creatures multiply, albatross on albatross, one velvet skirt on another. The thin boned Indian in Peru breathes that last air allowed her. We carry these troubles with us, as she wears all her skirts, pleat on pleat, as soon we will have to wear our houses, beds, dishes, heat, and travel, like snails, across the poison.

Do you remember your lovers? There are too many to take with me, several forgotten, one name never learned, and once, I lived with a man five years, and afterwards, I could barely remember the bed. Did he sleep on his side? Or his back? Did we make love in the morning? What was the taste of his breath? I want to remember the woman who kept a pear by her bed to sweeten her mouth, and I envy Eve her single apple. And there was the Indian woman, from San Nicolas Island, who lived in solitude for eighteen years, and being rescued, died.

I am afraid of your touch. Aren't we better off with our profligate servitude, attached to all our creatures, and knowing nothing remains in the nest. Have you seen the one the jay abandoned under my window? It sits in the weather. New birds won't settle the old nest and the old straw won't do. No jays take the gray twigs from this old house to build another. I think the wind will take it first, and another nest will be built in its place elsewhere, and I'll worry about the cats again, watch the squirrels battle the birds, and wonder where my loyalty lies in the war for survival.

Which do you favor? The fur or the feathered? Do you take both in your arms? The last owl hoots in the trees, surviving among the escaped parakeets, while the neighbors hunt the coyote, the deer nibbling in the suburban orange trees, the offending raccoon, and other mischievous creatures, lost, like the migrating geese, wandering too far, looking for a place to land, losing their bearings.

It it were only a question of whales, or only of Indians. If it were only a question of women. If it were only half the creatures of the world needing saving, perhaps, we could put out our arms. If only something would act against this increase, if all that which multiplies would diminish. If it were only milk at my breast, and not cancer. If it were only a child in the womb, and not cancer. If the wild growth were only geranium and morning glory, if it were not lovers sliding from us like dead skins, if it were not the multiplication of losses, if we could find one place to make a stand, if the entire world were not in danger. If we could stop now, at this instant, as we're walking, and watch the ocean leap up at us and return constant, we could probably put out our hands. But there are more in our fingers than whales, more in them than women, more threatened by extinction, than we encompass.

We put out our hands, but we can not close the circle. So we walk on the beach, begging the night to hide the creatures we love. We walk on the beach, our hands at our sides, thousands of miles between us, the whales calling from the sea.

The Indians Call It Heart
(On the Occasion of the Nuclear Disaster at Three Mile Island)

For Steven Kent

You say you had a dream and later found yourself thick in the mud of your sleep. In the dream, you did not wet your feet, but later the mud rose high, and you were afraid it would pull you in. But in the dream, we travel further than the fist. There is a door in the universe, we can not find marching. I have given up soldiering, even being a warrior of the heart, my chosen profession, and am learning to be a handmaiden and a keeper of beasts.

You say, "The beginning is the heart. Heart leads to tribe." I say, "Behind it the spirits grow fur and howl in unison." If at the moon, it is because she shows herself only to their eyes. The bitch is ill and the wolf cub howls day and night, sending out her calling on the radiant air. Within some miles, another wolf, hearing her, learns to climb trees to escape the zoo.

The wild beasts find each other in songs we can not understand. Do you fear wolves? Call them wild? They live in packs. They can not live alone. The wolf cub eats the food from the dog's mouth, then licks her wounds as well. Separated, they sing together. In the night, songs meet and whirl about each other. The eddy in the air is such a dance. Loneliness has this inevitable shape of hands.

This is the struggle between what can not be seen and what can not be seen. This morning, we watch the invisible poison burning. What is dead can be a raging growth and we have placed the cancer of our bones into the ground, and it comes back to us again, one feeding the other; we call it breeding, we are willful even in our language. Core burns toward core. Yet hell is not in the center of the earth, but in our marrow. What radiates from us is the lethal breath of the dead heart.

After you dreamed the canyon, you found that holy ground. There people make bowls from the soil. It's a simple process. Earth mixed with water. Fire which will not burn without air. The elements partner in a cosmic dance. You know the story of our origins: In these dark times, we must turn again to such simplicity and begin with that same clay, fashioning graven images with our awkward paws until some breath moves in them again. I have heard the spirits in the night bruising for lack of a house.

The invisible comes in two shapes. While the dark we will not see charges us with rage, the wind, at the same moment, smears the air, yellow, with the full pollen of the pine. During my walk, a neighbor tells me she smuggles lemons across the border, and I see the sycamore showing the first green in little nests of leaves. The dog, dying of cancer, her mammary duct removed, pushes her nose through the fence to comfort the whelp. Two doves sit, impeccable, on the wall, while the wind stirs the Japanese plum tree, leaves the true color of blood. Nights I have watched the dog dream and still did not believe.

Think of the dream as dove. A leaf in her mouth. Herald. What has she seen? What waters does she cross? Believe in the leaf, you will not drown. I dreamed a rain dance once and also knew the dances against the demons well, but now I do not know the steps we need even without my shoes.

They say, defeat came to the Indians when the ghost dance ceased. I'll tell you what Emma Goldman said: "If there's no dancing at the revolution, I'm not coming." Help me to find the dance against this terrible death.

Threnody For Camellias

*And rich folks were escorted through
like tourists, with adolescent girls
staring at us while we washed like Jews
[a dozen of us naked in a shower]*

— from *Take Me Back to Tulsa,* by David Ray

The one pale with age, the one who drew stings, the broken one who fell away, the discarded one, the crushed one, pressed flat as a flower between leaves of a cattle car, the one soft as stamens and humming, the one erect as pistils and unbending, the one still rosy as dawn, the streaked one and the two, one clasped on the other, are dead. All of them, in that shower, that deadly spring.

In the morning, I see the camellia collapse onto the breakfast table. Still, I say, there is meaning somewhere in the universe. Once, a shadow, sharp as the dark, pierced me, once there was something to remind me of life, once something insisted, was upright as the leaves of camellia, persisted audaciously as hardy and knobby camellia buds, never falling, never open. Once, something poignant as the bare stem of camellia, stabbed me in the heart.

This morning, the sight of the camellia holds me. A camellia entrenched against a wall cannot run, cannot escape the snip, cannot fly into the wind, can only bend. The camellia says, we must refuse all miracles requiring the sacrifice of camellias. Even in the face of resurrection, we must refuse to trample the million camellias. The skies so bitterly red with camellia snow.

We can not sweep all the millions and millions of murdered camellias into the funeral song of a single bloom. We can not presume that the abrupt loss of this one camellia, or the happenstance prohibition of camellias, or the official refusal to issue permits for camellias, even the suicide leap of this gift of camellia, the splattered petals splayed upon a wooden table, the call to witness the camellia soul, so alert in the morning, fading from the broken flower, we can not presume this loss is as grave as the deliberate slaughter, one day, of all camellias. It isn't equatable, isn't utterable in the same breath, with the extinction of camellias, with the disappearance of the shadow of camellias in a rain that never fell, with the loss of the dream, the memory of camellias, their pale lashes, all their wide staring eyes.

During the middle ages, when the German town of
Luebeck was under siege, there was no food at all.
The people invented marzipan, a bread of almond
paste, sugar and rose water, which helped them
survive.*

During World War I, when the German soldiers
occupied Vilna, the hungry people entertained
themselves with tales of rare and exotic foods. My
mother, who was a small child, asked her mother
what marzipan was, and my grandmother answered,
"Oranges."

Oh, come and hear this dream of oranges and siege,
This dream of almond paste and hunger.
Tell my mother, she is hungry
For the dreams of the approaching soldiers
Tell those soldiers, my mother
Has never seen an orange.

Here we are together in the same dark night
And no one with a sweet crumb on her tongue
And all the thorny shadows filled with roses.

Tell the soldier, my mother
Will have round breasts like breads,
Tell my mother, the soldier with dark eyes
Is even younger than her brother.

When there is war,
All the soldiers lie down in the cold
Under the white flag of a dream.
Please cover the dead with orange blossoms.

My mother never dreamed
The young soldier's mouth was sticky with sweets,
Oh, his almond eyes.
Oh, her little breasts like orange flowers.

And all the children rocked to sleep
To lullabies of *rusinkes* and *mandlen,*
And all the hungry children rocked to sleep
To lullabies of raisin dreams and almonds.

And all the dead maidens asleep among the oranges,
And all the dead soldiers asleep among the roses.

> ** Thanks to Micky Remann for telling me this
> story.*

Eve is the first to know desire.

Eve is the first. She can not be alone. She carries his bone within her. Fashioned out of a rib. He has a hole in his side while she is built upon him. He is empty. She encloses him.

Perhaps it wasn't an apple, but blood oranges. Or pomegranates. Something which stained the hands and reddened the mouth.

They came out of the flesh, out of the wound, opening themselves into mouths. Astonishments.

With her teeth, she violated the fruit as she had been broken into, as Adam had been broken into first. But he would have no part of it again. The first and last man to give birth.

Eve spoke with the snake moving under her skin. It was the rib alive within her.

When she first saw the tree, she knew only that it was laden with apples and forbidden. As he had forbidden her to know him. Was he the tree then? Yes, he was also forbidden.

She walked around the tree, admiring its shape, its texture. There it was twisted, there it was bent, and there it was gnarled. It was only a tree. Those were only apples. One should not expect anything. There was nothing to expect. There was nothing to desire. She would have to invent desire.

She looked at her body. She saw she was made in his image. There was not a single mark upon her. She was immaculate. It filled her with terror. She reached out for the scars of apples.

Eve was not seduced by the serpent. She waited her time by the tree and when the serpent reached the upper branches where the fruit was, Eve spoke: "I will have that."

The apple was never intended for Eve. Eve plotted with the snake. She wanted to give Adam a piece of her flesh, a sliver of her bone to bear within him. She wanted to fill the hollow in his side with her own body. When she came to him with apple on her tongue, she prayed that he would not be able to resist her.

Adam was ashamed. Eve laughed. When she admired her own breasts, he covered her hair with withering leaves.

They stepped out of the Garden onto the hard dirt. The speed of the fall was a weight upon her breasts. They sagged from the momentum. In an instant, their bodies altered. The globes, breasts, cheeks, bellies, testicles, descended. Gravity imposed itself.

Eve said, These bodies are the only power.

A month later, there was blood on her hand for the first time. Barely a month out of the garden, she passed her hands between her legs and found them wet with a warm, flat smell, bitter and sweet, and clearly organic, a new smell from that part of herself which she opened voluntarily and defiantly. She smeared the blood on her hands and on his mouth.

Abel wasn't the first death or the first blood spilled. When he came out of her womb, he came out bloody. To come out, he tore her open. As she had been torn out of Adam. As if there could be anything without such violence.

Eve questions god. "Where are your birth pains?" she asks. "Were you afraid, god, to carry us in your belly?"

Eve says, it was because of the lamb. It was that god gave the lambs to Abel. Abel was the best beloved, the favorite and he was given the slaughter.

It was that god came to Abel, his mouth bloody like a wolf—the first teacher—and the grease and smell of burned flesh upon his tongue. His mouth already full of death. God came to Abel in such clothing, in such robes. And they were lovers.

God gave the lamb to her son so Abel might kill it and wash his hands in the blood. Because god loved him, it was said.

It was a terrible beginning. Cain was also her son. He had fruit on his hands. His mouth was scented with oranges from his own fields. She wept. Because Cain was her son as was Abel. Because Cain had suckled the longest. Because Cain also drew blood.

She never understood why Abel agreed to slaughter the lambs.

Cain was the first fool. He was the first fruit of her womb. He was the child of apples. He had brought corn, as an offering, to the god who laughed at him for not anticipating history. The same god who had already given Cain's father stones to eat and a promise of pain to his mother.

Cain was an innocent. Eve watched how slowly he grew into knowing. He had not eaten the apple. He could not learn everything at once and she could tell him nothing. She could give them nothing. Had she known, she would have laid in a store of apples for such terrible winters as were coming to each of her children.

They were in the field and her back was breaking from the rocks which had to be cleared before plowing. She collected all the stones she could lift and hurled them at heaven. She made a slingshot of her heart. But she didn't have the reach and the stones fell in a great rain.

Abel was full of pride. Grain flowed through Cain's hands. Under this sun, he could bake bread without fire. God emerged from behind the tree, calling for burnt offerings, for flesh dancing in the fire.

Abel kneeled before him. Abel became the best beloved. Cain turned his back. He was the firstborn. Eve's son. While Abel was ecstatic before the fire.

Eve encircled Cain with her arms a last time against the god's laughter, but the fraternity of bloodletting extended. The line of blood scarred each of her sons and she could not stop it. It was no wonder, she thought, that god had not allowed her daughters.

Eve says, she is the enemy of this god. She says, he takes her by force. He takes her in the night and without knowing. He takes her in silence and invisibility. As a ghost. Without a body. Adam becomes a thief and steals the child from Eve's legs even as it is covered with her blood. He smears the blood on his mouth and calls the son, *ben Adam*. She says, when she can no longer protect her son, god leads him to the slaughter.

Eve names all her children who will be taken by god. Abel was the first god stole and Cain was the second. After Isaac, she became wary. She hid her son in the bulrushes, but god discovered him. She was not deceived when god spared some of her sons in the terrible bloodletting of the firstborn. She would not distinguish between one child and another.

She bides her time under the rain of plagues. She will not fight to the death. She can not kill even for her sons' sakes. She pours her own blood onto the ground. She is studying how to make her own war without murdering. She says she invents life and this god invents death, and they are enemies. Soon, she says, she will bring everything down and end the bloodletting.

Eve says she wants to enter Adam as Adam enters her, she wants to open the wound where the rib was and crawl inside. She wants to be a bone in return for his bone. She wants to be one with him. She wants him to be one with her. One inside the other. She wants to end the wars.

She says, Adam, you search out the forbidden Tree of Apples, you pick apples for us to eat.

Against earwigs and sow bugs,
against flies, fleas, and ants,
against spiders,
against aphids, against fruit flies,
against beetles,
against rats and gophers,
against rabbits, against coyotes,
deer and wolves...

Fire bombing the hills, the flaming gel singes the
creosote then explodes, trotting down the brush and
galloping up. Fight fire with fire until there is nothing
left to burn.

The doctor suggests radiation or excavating the chest
cavity, pulverizing the masses and placing the
chemical charges in the scrapped out site. It will burn
into tissues for weeks; the blood cells will die too.

Feathers blow down among cinders. It is not certain
when, if ever, the land will be habitable. When
lightning cracks the tree open, we lament the act of
god, meaning it is random.

War is orderly. Soldiers are trained to keep time in
formation. The men prisoners from the local work
camp, in red and yellow uniforms, pull fire hoses in
straight lines supervised by captains seated in the
polished fire trucks gleaming like apples in the early
summer light.

It is the solstice. Our days will be shorter. The Vietnam vet says: "When you work the lines, as I have, and you watch them douse the trees with gasoline and put a torch to it to set a backfire, you have to ask yourself, do they know what they are doing?"

The surgeon's instruments are displayed in precise rows, the exact calculations for chemotherapy require only a laboratory and a computer, but not the alignment of the planets. The lunar calendar says: "Chaos steers all things."

It's dawn. The third day. The chain saw wails in the hills. Helicopters survey the area, second chance for the pilots from Nam. The men align themselves with the coordinates of north and south.

The land is burning bright yellow and red. The can reads: "Against flies. Do not contaminate feed and foodstuffs. Young calves can pick it up and lick it. Do not use in homes or where milk is processed. Use only in areas inaccessible to food production. Do not use in restaurants or where food is exposed. Exposed surfaces are hazardous to birds and wildlife. Use with care in areas frequented by wildlife or adjacent to any body of water."

She has a choice only of different poisons. It is said that the gods are erratic. Prayer, therefore, is ineffective, not indicated, except for ritual purposes or when the fire sweeps back against you, and it gets hot. Then you are permitted to swear, God damn.

Flying insect killer in the red and yellow can kills
fast. Works

against flies,
against mosquitoes, gnats,
flying moths, against wasps,
hornets and German cockroaches,
against waterbugs, roaches,
earwigs and spiders.

Caution Do not use Warning Avoid Keep out of
reach of
Fast knockdown   Fast kill.

And today the rain comes. A small knocking on the skylight at night, as if something mechanical is aflutter or a shy animal is cleaning its home.

The earth remembers, but not easily. At first the crust is adamant, lets nothing in, the water flows down the sides. Only gradually does the soil open, become permeable, let the rain slip between the stones. Then the clay slides over the bones of rock.

The mystery of rain. The sky, transparent and miraculous, falling toward the earth. The sky, given to us, offering itself, in the form of rain. The god descending, to be taken up or taken in.

When I was ten, a storm was fierce enough to wash my hair in the rain, the water breaking over my head and streaming white down my body, a wraith of white foam about my ankles. I kept my face toward the sky long after the soap had disappeared, for the hammer of water upon my naked body.

I have been afraid to pray for rain. I do not know if we retain the right, given that we set fires in all our footprints. And I want to make no promises we can not keep.

Once rain came to me in a dream in the form of dancers. I awakened frightened, but the next week I danced the rain dance, and then it did rain. It was a satisfying coincidence. And then it rained again and continued to rain. And rain. I tried to forget the dream. I didn't dance again and didn't call for rain.

Another time, it rained for days. The hill slid against the house. The water seeped in through the walls. In the morning, it seemed as if the bed was afloat, or the room itself was a solar barque taking us to our death. To die by water is said to be a gift of the gods. Again, I didn't know if I should pray for sunlight.

Each summer, the river is brown and warm as the beginning of time at Canyon de Chelly. The river is always knee deep where the sheep graze the river grasses. But last summer, the river was dry as the canyon walls. The juniper drooped at the edge, the pinion pine parched, the wind dusty and unrelenting moaned through the stunted milpa. Bears came down from the hills looking for water. I asked for the dream to return as a sign, though I was afraid. But the dream did not return, and I saw no dancers, not even in the clouds.

Today the rain returns. The mud slides. Steam blows off the wet fence during intermittent moments of sun. Small green grasses arise at the side of the road. Mist hovers about the edges of the mountains. The canyon glides again toward the sea.

The wolves break open the door, dry themselves at the hearth. Little field mice scurry through the cabinets. The frogs which have lived in the closet move outside, singing. Bulbs break through the soft earth, scent of narcissus, glimpses of hyacinth.

In the beginning, after the flood there was a rainbow. Now, during the drought, this sweet interval of rain. But the question remains: Do we have a right to pray for rain? And what, then, can we offer before we take take in the rain with our dry roots and open mouths when the fires we are setting are seething on the horizon?

Mating

We who no longer live on the land dream about it. When the rains come as they did this year, I want to go out in the streets to pull up the pavement so the waters can enter. I think I know what ought to be separate and what needs to join. We cover the earth as if she were also ashamed. I want to undress her with my bare hands.

The little pots, the little tubs, the little basins, the cement rivers full of sacred water break in the tremor of the earth's breath. When the ribs expand, she will not bear the stiff girdle we impose. She carries us, but not the concrete weight. The buildings sway, everything permanent we erect is tenuous, only the erratic beauty of the tree, only what sways, breaks into leaves, what sheds, stands. I see the streets break up, potholes and broken cement. It cheers my heart. The city looks like certain countries I've traveled in—what I thought was disrepair were the elements reaching out to join again. The slashed hills refuse to hold themselves erect, the houses slide into the sea, all the earth scars mend themselves. What has been set apart, seals. What has been sundered, heals.

In the night, I hear the rain falling. Sitting with a friend, I think about the sea trying to enter the sand. I think about mud. It's a metaphor. The universe is running. I'm sure of it. I've waited all night for this moment of hands thrust like trees into the dawn. The stars may fall into the sea. The clouds stretch out, black bellies pressed soft onto the earth. I cheer the river rising out of the cement bed, the mud pushing down, everything moving in its own current, and the world gliding out from under our feet.

There isn't any solid ground, nothing to fix our bearings on. Even the poles shift. It is as it ought to be.

We have had more than forty days of rain. A friend says: "We are not going to be lucky again and have miracles performed for us." This is not a warning, but the reclaiming of a lost land. The dove is not coming back with an olive branch to save us from what we need. The ark founders and splits apart. The mountain peak at Ararat buries its nose in the sweet water. Though it is said, rivers do not flow up the mountain, still the river hungers for the air. We're all the river caught in green time, struggling through the wet roots, one water changing into another, the rains coming, the entire tide of the universe singing.

Each of us carries the light and the water which makes earth our mother. When the rains come, the dreams run and the roots take them in. The sea moves into the sand, each drop married to a grain and passing into the dance. The sea's a white fury chasing what opens to it. I am ready to travel. It is time to move on. One wet foot after another, toward the mother sand, calling the tides, bringing our houses down.

E d e n

It was already a garden,
It always was,
And now these small preserves
At the edges of exile.

Our frantic assertions,
"It wasn't our fault,"
"It isn't our fault,"
When we know it is.

Everything, everything rises out of the haze or snow toward the bluebell and falls away. Seed, stem, calyx, petal, flower, fruit, rise and then all fall; seed falls, stem falls, calyx falls, petal falls, flower falls, the stalk, the dry leaf, even the dying falls away from the point of blue. The flower is long gone, the light which knew it disappears. But in the mind, that locus of the awakening of the night remains tattooed upon the memory, the way a glacier persists in the sun and grinds down whatever it rides upon.

The rain has returned. Color washes out of the trees into the ochre mud. The eucalyptus easily turns gray and the grass seeks brown. There in the orchard, the remaining yellows and small oranges dull before they drop in the wind, remind me how swiftly innocent color drifts away, withdraws its inner light in this winter rain. Now it is metal that gleams; the broken white flank of the van has an eerie shimmer, the car, also aging and scratched, manages a stark, even defiant light; these twin moons illuminate the day lit yard.

In the window, the astonishment of blue glass against the gray sky persists even when the mind cannot imagine anything but the drab clouds and the light which will not hold before it slides away. In the instance of the window, however, everything moves toward the blue, and the landscape converges in that point of sea and sky.

A photograph. Paris in the rain. A memorial. The dark bronze will last a thousand years in the dull light. The steel skeleton of the Camps grows out of barbed wire, thorn out of thorn. Spectrum of the broken light consumed at the still point where no color can exist.

Did the Beginning cohere out of night or out of day? Is it blue which is the first color from the stars or did the world cleave to itself out of fire and break into those yellows, reds, and oranges which wrap themselves even now about the body of wood without making any alteration of the day?

In the fireplace, wood offers another kind of light to the persistence of rain. Reading the fire, I see my people ablaze, one log, one body, against another. The more they lean, the faster they burn. Against the blackened iron, the triumphant yellow flames. Then I have to look away to the blue glass in the window and the thin light coming through from needles of platinum stars behind the fog and I am grateful for the time which stretches without end beyond my own life. Those colors of fire I know too well if not firsthand. In certain countries of northern Europe, the flare of that infernal light spread like a pall, a noxious fog for years, a palette of black, red, orange, of carbon and smoke while human fat fed the bloody flames.

We saw the small lake which held the light as we walked in the rain, but held it only as metal takes it on, and then the fog drifted across the hills pausing before sage, oak, gray stalks—last season's yellow mustard grass—obliterating all.

I go to the end of the world. First color leaves. Then what? The bougainvillaea which blazed upon the fence, died back in the cold and wears the sky like a shroud. I make no predictions about what can or will endure. Birds hover silently under the brambles; even the music appears to be gone.

And I wonder about this poem. Who is it I am trying to awaken with this spectre of blue? And how? And to what?

I do not know if the trees and brush drift away in the fog, if they retreat from each other as we do with the coming of the dark, and as the rain lifts, remain just a little bit further apart. Safety, perhaps, only in the long run of the stars toward an impossible and necessary horizon where everything is so distant that nothing is with anything but itself. And the heart, also, fleeing in pieces, away from itself, astonished by—even in awe of—the electronic spin of its parts.

"You are lonely," he said. "You are afraid." But I denied it. Pieces of broken glass are not afraid. Kindling, the gathered twigs and branches, the cut logs are not afraid. I swore, "I need nothing, want nothing I can not give to myself, was not, am not, will never be afraid."

Had he looked back at the pillar of salt—tincture of blue in the dying light silhouetted against the flames, corona of hell on her head, like a figure of ash before the burning of cities—the mineral which she had joyously become, wouldn't he also have implored, "Let it rain." And welcomed the silence of it, cobalt rain, the blue waters, death rising, the quiet of it. Everything moving toward the blue or away.

Defeats

You come home from the first battle, the bandage about the heart, dust in the palm of the hand more withered than the earth. In the ravines, the water drives mercilessly, and then the dry season leeches a great red dust. The geography in the flesh, an old folded map, tearing where it has been opened, worn, and where you've been, without knowing the four directions, the white bandage, flopping and dirty, or a gray *rebozo* bound about the breast.

When you stumbled, the clay embedded in the shoes, soil of one country passing customs to another; whatever you carry—plants, meat, liquor—is forbidden. Barbed wire fences, broken glass on walls, clanging church bells and heavy iron gates against the sky, while hidden the sacristan compels obedience with a bell rope, heavy pull of time, authority in the terrible heat, in the desire for rain, and sins, common as fleas, in the plaza.

The *hidalgo* denied his mother, *La India,* but told you he went on his knees, *de rodillas,* across La Basilica de Guadalupe, 'our saint,' the slow shuffling before Her. When he was young, skinned knees, stigmata, and now he pushes her onto her fours, elbows and knees, and mounts you, quivering like the lean and hungry curs. "If you have a stone," Morena said, "the dogs are stilled," and in the fearful yard, she howls the empty midnight, the astonished bitch.

In every crevice, Mexican clay, that red earth, or blood between the legs, menstrual or wound, the wad between the legs removed, blocked entrances to old ruins, stones pushed aside, the first invaders, thieves. Wrapped in bandages, the ancient dead do not resist sufficiently, a pyramid between the thighs yawns reluctantly, old blood bursts out or new.

Rust stains, fire clay hardening, soil hardpacked under the plum shade, turkeys pecking the earth clean, and the old palm brooms sweeping. Rain carves steps in the street, and in the assault, hands, quick as machetes, husk the earth, and over all the patina of old clay disintegrating, and beneath that, shards, shattered vessels, beheaded temples, broken images, footprints, ashes. Everyone is looking for treasures, clay figurines smiling, ancient hags, *las diosas, la luna,* also hurled out of the fire into the universe to turn about the sun.

Long after she's abandoned, the men return and find the dust heavy as musk. She could not keep her distance. They break the force field, the balance of nature teeters on its axis, heavy boots walk where they will over the altars of *la luna, las diosas,* collecting fingers, for the museum, bits and pieces, the torsos of Xochiquetzal, Xochimilco, Tlazacotl, Xipe, Coyolxauhqui, *la diosa, la luna,* is entered again.

Habits older than hoes honored in the resistance to fences. "Territory calling us," they say, "in her wild voice." The *hidalgo* says, "*Machismo* is never against the woman," gripping his dinner knife in a fist. Where the wolves wander, chicken wire buckles before yellow eyes. In the north, the coyote, in the south, the jaguar, slither across the pelvis of the earth. It used to be she gave an invitation in the spring, but now the maiden is not permitted her annual return. The hag, earth, may grumble, but he plows, when he plows, where he plows. *La luna* heaves, barren and powerless, he breaks into her as well, and in the battle—the bruise on your arm, did you fall? Ochre murals, red traces of sacrifices.

On the road, the two volcanoes, the Sleeping Woman, Ixtacchihuatl, and El Popo, lie in a snow sleep, inviolate through the curtained mercy of clouds. Later, one of them, *el gringo barbudo*, or the *hidalgo*, says, he mounted her with ropes and pitons, climbing to the very crown while Anaberta, *la bruja*, tried to scale El Popo, but, being untrained, remained at the snow line, the circle of ropes, an empty epaulet upon her shoulder.

Earlier the cards say, 'danger,' they say, 'beware.'
You say, he endangers you, the American salesman,
pouting *conquistadore*, pack on his back, trading
new gold, new gods, *huipiles, sarapes, ponchos,
rebozos, mota*. He's blond and bearded, the Huichole
call him, 'brother,' teach him the shaman story,
peyote puckers his mouth, brings dreams of
Broadway, Saks Fifth Avenue, the big time. He says
"Come, you, Morena, the dark one, we go, we go
Guatemala, we go Huatla, we go Oaxaca. Yes?" He
says, "You, me, the dark one, who speaks the
language, she go too, she speak English, Spanish, she
speak Maya, she speak Nahuatl, she speak Quiche,
we go *pulque, hongos, indios, telas, mercados*. What
you want? *Yerbas? Curanderos?* I buy you world."

You clutch your heart, take the spine out, *maguey*
needles, the cards say 'beware,' you turn your back,
make a circle to call the rain, yet fearing all the
elements, the way alone is better; the cliffs of
Tepoztlan are sharp and steep. From the pyramid,
watching like a sentinel, the owl of night hoots,
cuidado. You do not glance at him, his gods are
daggers, lethal as old spears. *La bruja* warns, your
body is in danger, you pulled the virgin card Dona
Anaberta whispers, dark eyes, the moon, *escondida*
the tarot, *La Virgen*, "don't be manhandled." A
horse whinnies, Morena says, "It's the full moon."
All the dogs exclaim, *peligro*, the night undresses
you, fold in the *camison* of damp and lonely sleep.

The book says: *"Los antiguos mexicanos acostumbraban sangrarse casi todas las carnes del cuerpo en actos de penitencia or autosacrificio que hacian en honor de sus dioses. Utilizaban entre otros instrumentos espinas vegetales."*

A series of openings. The altars where the hearts are torn away. As many as 10,000 a day. The sun is hungry, the heart leaps, Mexican jumping beans, grasshoppers fried in the market. "If you eat them, you'll never leave Oaxaca," the *hidalgo* said. Holy locusts, chalice engraved on their backs, do god's work, eating the *milpa*, the cornfield, the corn. The land crackles with sacrifice and invaders.

The insects suck voraciously, huge welts, pyramids raised, blood suckers or blood letting, *pulgas, chinches*. The women pack a poultice, white powder, cool cool, against the hot blood, they say 'cluck cluck,' cooing, the hot sun bears down, chiles burn, green and violet red, the doctor says, "The red ones, especially, are good for the heart."

The book says: *"En efecto, cinco eran los tipos de sacrificio: por extraccion del corazon, el gladiatorio, por asaeteamiento, el de fuego, y por decapitacion."*

And even earlier, before the journey, one came to her on his *norteamericano* knees looking for sacrifice, begging for chains, for whipping, for her lunar mercilessness, calling her, Coyolxauhqui, *la luna diosa*, who wanted to murder her mother after a similar shame. Her heart turns over like the soil, when she turns her back, he crawls, wet and cold, into the bushes, *la culebra* cures anemia, cancer, he is colder than reptiles; there's no heat. "I will never sleep with a man I do not love," you swear, his shadow slipping toward the other snakes. She is untouched, and dances like the virgin under *la luna* which gives her no protection.

After every encounter, the women, cluck cluck, the chickens pecking in the yard, poultices and feathers, the virgin is fifteen, *la fiesta rosa*, the blood, pure and pale, we are the godmothers of the cake, frosted, like the snowy hair of Ixtacchihuatl. Pat pat; the women make *tamales, arroz, frijoles, mole, dulce, tortillas* under the ceiling where the snake skin hangs, *piel de culebra*, for healing, for cancer, for anemia, for blood—*"es una gran cosa para la sangre"*—and beside it, the bouquet of hot chiles, also for the heart.

Encounters in the marketplace, the arterial chiles pulse on a white plate beside the *hidalgo, el rubio*, from Tehuantepec where tall and strong women display peppers in pyramids to the sun. These amazons of velvet and lace teach him war, he says, calling her, *"mamita."* He does not need a knife, not even a flint blade, only the night and the force of arms.

To peel a chile, put it in the fire. When it blisters, pull the skin off. The flesh remains, red stains like blood, run *picante*, into the corn, the savor of the chile remains and the fire helps you toward the seeds within. Your sign is Virgo, loss surrounds you in the five colors of maize, white, yellow, speckled, blue, red.

Bougainvillaea in all colors, blood over the wall, roosters and church bells, faded dawn breaking. "On Saturday night, the men kill each other," Morena says while the women walk in the shadows. The moon hides firecrackers, shotguns, knives, quick silver, *la culebra* in the grass, the transparent scorpion is the most deadly—the tail lunges and you're dead, you're dead, you're dead.

Her blood, the moon above, pulling your legs open, the struggle, he enters—you've never learned karate—and anyway—the knife—you haven't the strength. The snake poises, *culebra*, in the cunt, mouth, ass, biting.

You steal from the bed. What belongs to you is smeared upon the sheets, a stain you leave with him. The *hidalgo, conquistadore,* turns to press against the blood root, whispers, "*Te amo. Tu eres una mujer fabulosa.*"

Later, she falls running down the streets broken from so much water, steps down, or up, from the altar where the knife cut the heart out, the sun has to eat, heat, heat. The moon is hiding you against the wall, the dogs sleep under collapsed bougainvillaea, the chiles explode out of their dark skins, the blood between the legs, terra cotta pottery, these shattered figures discovered in the earth.

Red chiles, *grandes y pequenos*, red and rust colored, scorpion tailed *huipiles*, red, rust, blood colored *rebozos*, the *chile salsa*, the *mole*, the peppers ground fine, the red powder on the fingers, the flaming cockscomb crowing, the red fire rising.

The women go, 'cluck cluck,' they rub her body with oil, anti-venom, a poultice. They wash her, the *temezscal* woman beats her with *zapote* leaves against *los aires*. Your back is cold like the moon, the hags beat you till the steam rises, a mist against the sun, nothing can be seen of the Sleeping Woman. The sweat on her breast beading, the vapors rising, her skin rubbed clean, shining like the moon, the waters silver the night, the blood running clear, you can drink it, the well is good. The chickens peck the garden clean, the turkey hens gobbling the refuse, the cock preening his feathers, the red comb, like blood, falling between her legs.

The egg is full of poison. The yolk is buried. Her heart is beating beating. They pack a poultice of white clay, a seal, the kiln, the fire, the hard pottery, the goddess, *la diosa, la luna,* the laughing figurines. The flowers sweep over the walls. She is named Xochil, flower.

The rains come. The mud flows, blood, over the houses of the *conquistadores.* You come home. The women go 'cluck cluck,' they spin about you, little white eggs, they break open clean, the steam is white, the maize is yellow, the zapote leaves are fresh, new trees over old ruins. The old women grin, pat pat, *tortillas, tamales* wrapped carefully as bandages, *acostarte acostarte,* go to sleep, go to sleep, the gray *rebozo* binds her breast, a hammock hanging from the horns of the stark moon.

I have lived in the desert a long time, learning to love the cactus, to value the water stored in the Joshua tree. I claim the adopted land as something I remember. Bare green, bitter oil, the swollen testicles of goats, the gods born among the rocks, harsh and negligent, in their loving.

I come out of the desert and behind me are the hot winds. The desert is the earth, burning, by herself. The winds follow her with a force I love. They are the tent upon her hair.

Once the windows in my house blew out, the glass shattering as if a fire had entered. The sirocco, the mistral, the Santa Ana all make one mad.

When we met in the desert, we were wanderers. It appears, I danced the heat dance, following the whirl of the wind with the hip bone. When there is no water, invite the wind to stir the earth a little. Someone played the *dümbek*. Am I not a drum? Skin stretched tight, waiting. You and I barely spoke. You did not strike me with your palm. I could have worn a veil and caught you with my eye. When the earth is dry, even invited waters do not enter.

If in the daytime, I learn to love the desert, stare unblinkingly, caught by the mirror heat, still, I want the veil of rain upon the night's eye. In my sleep, the dreamer instructs me in the calling down of water. A simple dance: two little twofooted leaps and two little onefooted leaps. Repeat: two little twofooted leaps and two little onefooted leaps. Repeat:

I catch you with my eyes. The rains come heavy in the beginning of the year.

I come out of the desert. In secret, you tell me you are water. I have been waiting forty years for this. The wandering is over. I didn't strike the rock and no one says, "Die here, having seen the land toward which you were leading us."

I didn't strike the rock. I recognize the desert for what she is and love her for her loss. Once, I washed my hair in the absolute rain. Once I asked the rock for water, holding a shaman's stone, and the desert woman disappeared into the hide of a white calf.

You said: "Why come in from the rain? Why not stay here, remain wet?" My belly is wet from sweat. We rub against each other, making fire. But we are not stones. Perhaps the desert woman took the dry skins and put wine in them. Perhaps the goat appeared full of milk and piss. Perhaps a damp calf is born from the sand. Perhaps the mud is wet.

The rock opens to us. Everything we are, is water. Your sex is wet within me. We pull as currents on each other.

This rhythm is the tide. There is no water we haven't known. I feel the plunge of flying fish and the entire ocean lying between us shudders as the continental shelf expands. Reaching.

I remember indelible footprints on the sea. Seaweed on my mouth. I carry the taste of you like a vial of holy water.

We have been turning, you and I, in the intense dark seas which move in currents toward each other. Each turning in their own direction, slowly crossing the equator. Great beasts of water, like the black waves scraping the ocean body, pressing with relentless ease toward this white meeting. No one sees the storms under the sea. On the surface, an ordinary meeting of sea birds, a calm flower in the sea's hair, but underneath the waters, the shapes of leviathan love heave and throb in the cold, invisible depths.

Great water feet walk along the bottom of the ocean. Heavy elephantine currents, the dormant lust of astonished beasts, hippopotami, rhinoceri, great whales, sea serpents which have yet to be discovered. Everything has mass and intensity and hangs in the sexual urge. These great drums of flesh, this call of some terrible urgent nature, in the twist of deadly current.

And so we roll
    and the night passes
        and the dawn comes
        and the water
            turns.

The sea rises, altered, from its bed, from the great waves pounding into each other and presents the mystery of who is entered and who is entering. In the stake of one body on another, the elements win. The water spreads its thighs. A great cry, the inner thunder of fish persists, and the sea thrusts hips up and down, mountain ridges peaking, and whirls in white pelvic rocking toward the moon.

She said, we'll never fall in love again. I thought, I'll follow the body as a river, low for lack of rain, follows, still flowing, green and warm, warmer for the lack of water through the curving banks. Or I would follow the body like the ocean, the swell of tissues, the constant reminder of desire, the fullness from the rub of things against each other. We are all almost water and love increases us whether it finds us or not. Waiting for the ocean wave to spill, the blond and thoughtless boy plunged his body into a hole in the wave bringing it crashing down. Love doesn't happen that way; the waves persist.

She said, we'll never fall in love again, not any of us as I had said the same words years before in Greece. I had said, I'll never fall in love again, let the body take what it can. Making love in the soft Mediterranean at full noon with a stranger, I thought, I'll never fall in love again, this twitch of the body is the best that we can manage, the sea breaking over me, our bodies linked, shark on shark, in the gentleness of it. And days later, on a ferry from Piraeus to Brindisi, I thought, I'll never fall in love again, and followed a man in unmatched pants and coat until he followed me, and pressed himself against me, fucking, in a room too small to love in. I thought, I'll never, the waves tossed us against the rhythm of our own bodies, we rocked against the waves.

The sea always wins. It crests. You can plunge into the wave breaking it at its height or foot, a surfer puncturing the circular swell like a sleek whale, but the water closes up again behind the whale, and the swell continues a tense relentless crest. The swell of desire in the body maintaining itself like waves crossing the Pacific, sweeping relentlessly toward another coast, the underbelly of the sea moving with the urgent cry of tide.

She said, we'll never fall in love again, not any of us. Plunging, parting the water recklessly, without regard for the wave, seeking the camaraderie of molecule and flow, and in early morning, breaking into the air without announcement, walking without thought of that which opens for us, forgetting to ask permission of the fire before we split one flare from another, moving the coals and flames arbitrarily, and without notice digging the earth, the spade incising the surface without a 'by your leave'—these rude gestures do not serve us to enter the elements.

The dreams I had this week of being parted, sundered, exposed by some Moses issuing orders to the Red Sea, divided as the waters are split by a stone thrown into them, the air torn by bodies which pierce its fabric. My own body unraveling, unseamed, shabby from the discourtesy of entrances and exits, and needing to be mended. I become the seamstress of the waters, learning from the dolphin not to make love in the sea like rude divers in harpoon pursuit of anything which flashes, not charging against the waves, foam for foam. The dolphin has an agreement with the sea to seal the nest behind it as it exits.

I said, I'll never fall in love again. She said, we'll never fall in love again, not any of us. But we followed the body like a river, green and warm, nudging the bank. And swimming that afternoon, after the long walk down to the waters hidden by tall grasses, after we had thought we would never get to the banks of the green snake, for everything was high and dry, we found the water. Swimming cautiously, as if I were a maiden preparing to fall in love, respectfully asking the river god to let me enter, I knew we would fall in love again if we could honor the currents and enter the sea as the river does, mingling atom for atom. Allowing the body to suck in the new water, the waves building up in the retreat, and the new peak, desire, in the forward motion mingling sweet water into salt.

Empty Dachas

The morning woman watches the sun come up alone,
the dark sky lightening, her feet are cold, her heat not
sufficient, she knows loneliness because she sleeps in
socks, cold falling toward her like water from the
remote side of the bed. What buds survive this
winter? Snow on the pillow, the roaming herds eat
every piercing shoot.

Why buy flowers? I say the self is double and lilacs
are for the two of us. The cottonwoods are stripped
of bark. In the empty fields, the old horses are dead.

Without a lover, I wonder at the face in the mirror.
They used to bring two horses, at the very least, for a
wife. The body, the heart, each bears up well and is
deserving. I know about loving and though an expert
I'm unemployed, overqualified, no one is willing to
pay the price.

It's morning. No night as difficult as when everything
is fresh. The mare who survives the winter bears a
colt as a sign of coupling. Even in California, it's cold
gray, but two can still see other things, the remaining
pigeons and squirrels. My eyes alone do not dissolve
the sleep haze or dream population, nightmare and
paradise, alike, multiply lovers. We ride bareback
across the plain stampeding the mustangs.

On the way home, I think I am too tired to buy
flowers, only the florists advertise spring. For two,
deprivation is more difficult; life matters when there
is a witness.

I am without a lover—is there some shame in it? They say the stallions are gone, the plains devoured by a strange snow which permits no survivors. I am in Russia after the war when all the men are killed and the women learn to live without. The tundra spreads across the continents, resurrecting the land bridge in the Bering Straits. The cold moves down and frosts the sheets.

Do I sit in a little room after the factory day pretending it is ok to have a glass of tea alone watching the steam rise on the frosted windows, straightening the lace tablecloth, polishing the silver because an Aunt is coming on Sunday? The friend I meet at the street corner, huddled in her fur coat, white breath greeting me, do we talk carefully about afternoon spring flowers—morning flowers wilt when the deaths come—and will we share a dacha where it's warm by the Black Sea far from these ice floes, and how do we count the years?

I think this is the year the men died. Doesn't it seem there are less of them, so many women without, and all the men with women? They say boy babies have less stamina and fewer are born and men die earlier, the women surviving them and the horses. And there is the death of the spirit, that war we don't talk about; it wipes out millions.

I write erotic poems, it's difficult without the male muse, some wild animal to carry me four legged across a prairie. Love is impossible outside the body, the one heart pulsing is not the same as one hand clapping. I can not write the memory I only ride in dreams.

But, unwillingly, I remember one morning with clarity. You showed me a shell the glaciers had not buried. The sky was in the room among the hyacinths we had bought coming home, After dawn we looked out of speckled windows, horses stomping in the snow, opened the glass to a brisk day zero weather. It didn't matter. The sun was across the street. We knew how to keep warm. Heat is strategic in Russia, men and women, in the same sleeping bags, on the front lines.

SHADOW LETTERS:
Self Portrait of a Woman Alone

This persistent search for the answer is perhaps in
itself a constant flight from wonder.
— Albert Einstein

Women alone get the pickings from others' lives. Yet gleaners served a function. Look how faithful Ruth was to Naomi.

These months we have been out of phase. Two of the fourteen moons of Jupiter, we do not turn at the same speed though we keep our orbit. You say you carry me in your heart over any distance. But what crosses these dead seas?

Since I have had to go out of the gates of the city to fight for love, I have named myself 'Warrior.' I am not tired, but have lost the ability to win. This day is called retreat. On my walk, broken foundations of deserted houses built only with what the mountains offer. In this desert, let me find a house of my own with a fireplace of stone. If I must be alone, let it be with the elements.

When we first met, you had been drumming in the dry hills. Yesterday, I drummed alone at the crest. The student of the Kalahari said, "The desert healers are men though some women have made that journey into the other world." Men can't heal unless the women sing. Men drum and women sing. Women singing for each other as well.

In the Kalahari, the older women build a nuptial house of sticks and then the couple lies down. If I would do that for you, now that you are not alone, it is because your singing has eased me. Otherwise, I do not know what sacred is.

When I asked, the I Ching answered, 'Gathering Together.' I can find nothing but lupine and dry twigs. Living alone, I must provide my meat and my protection. Territory says, I should become a huntress. You say, we are past the age of Artemis, and custom says, it is women who gather and the men who hunt. I go across the desert with empty hands. The hawks circle overhead. Nothing remains.

Cape Cod: Caitlin

Two days wondering what I will write to you.
Hoping to read something in these letters of tea
leaves and divining by the footprints of birds. The
crystal turns slowly in the alphabet of light. In this
room, the windows steam over, then bead. The drops
of water running down are postcards from the
universe. I can't read the messages. I have no
patience, never learned to knit, to twist long hours
into wool, even to keep warm. I do not know how
hemp holds ships in line.

Today I walk the dunes. Tomorrow, I return to
find my own tracks and follow them again. A friend
says, "Your journey is going home again." At dawn
the dunes say, "No one has been here before."
Everything disappeared as a man might into your
hair.

I am wandering down to water. I was born by the
sea, but my father was not a sailor. I do not know
how to live out in my hand what comes to me in
storms. These days I have had to learn north and
bitter and fjord.

I take the earth in my mouth. Welcome mad girl
who eats soil. I saw the wind's nest on the
promontory. There is more light here in the gray sky
than broken into colors, and the trees spread
themselves secretly across the darkness. I think you
know these distances of sea, moor and plain. It is not
night, but the gray implacable dawn calling me to
truce as the tide always calls the sun.

I think you're blond through dealing with this
harsh light. All fishermen are the colors of salt. Dark
mariners drown. The men I've loved have been the
color of rope.

Gather me into your stout nets.

Cambridge: Joyce

In the dream, it is I who give birth. You know how birth is. It can not be interfered with. The body has its own necessity which does not ask permission of the mind. Now in my house, the wolf bitch digs a den in the darkest corner and howls to her non-existent pup. Soon, the vet says, she will bring milk to her emptiness. Birth does not require progeny. We have a right to nurture nothingness.

Afterwards, in my dream, I am the one who gives birth. But when we meet, it is your daughter I see born on film. What comes out of us is for all our eyes. You could show birth to me once more and then again. The entire night passed with her emergence. You say the film was a call to what you had lost.

In the dream, afterwards, it is I who give birth. The birth is always the same. The child is invisible and must be taken by the hand. This is about hands.

In the cold streets, you put your hand in the pocket of my coat when we meet after twenty years. The door of your house opens to me as if it were never locked. I have returned to my beginnings in order to set out again. What I took with me from my childhood was forgetfulness. What you had in your palm was pain. As children, we stood outside the circle with each other.

To come home, I must learn where I first saw my own footsteps. At fourteen, I had a double loneliness of the body. You didn't know about my wandering at night. We shared the daytime, but after midnight, I roamed the beach learning the dialect of the sea. Later, I gave my body to lovers, hoping to drown. Here the ocean is wild, aggressive and merciless. My hair is silver. We have never known each other as women before.

I live in the shade of trees broad at the base like women who open themselves to oxen and buffalo. Where you live, the trees are slim as your daughter. The birch is shy and about to be given in marriage. The eucalyptus says, "Your silver hair is older than mine." My body is an old whore and the moon pulls me. In the restaurant, my friend says, "You can't go home." The old dog will die of the whelp's need.

Twenty years ago, you thought I had betrayed you when I had a child. Now you are ready. The old dog is dying. Yesterday, we cut out her breast. In her last moments, she and I are more than sisters. I say, I don't believe in symmetry or trying to create beauty out of pain. The young wolf will not be alone. Her blood tells her, "Run in packs." I also howl the night in the cold bed.

What can we count on after twenty years? The ocean. And our ability to walk alone. I am reduced to this belief.

Chatham: Judith

You're so blond, fishing without a hut through the holes in the ice. Places we can't ever go again. Shacks boarded against the wind we bring. Deserted villages turning their backs to the sea. Places we've met our lovers.

On the phone, you say, there is a thaw. The snow falls here where it never snows, does not stay on the ground, swirls to show me where the wind is and the shape of its mouth.

You said, let us play The Fool. I have been foolish and call it wandering. I don't go far enough. At my age, it is hard to be hungry and blistered. You're North of me, but I've gone as far as any of my people, with the wind always to my back. It is cold and my face is lined as the rock confronting the coast. The tower light turns even during the day and the sea horn hums through my bones. Seas high and gray. Again it snows. And again it snows. This is a National Preserve, but what is saved is emptiness.

You say, your work goes well. Work is my only remaining house. After our visit, the lake was beginning to thaw. When I entered your room, you were waiting with a bottle of wine.

These letters are about loneliness and persistent attempts to eat alone with grace. The meal is possible if I imagine I'm beautiful. About handsome women— one assumes they have choice.

In my dream, the wall becomes a door, strangers enter, call me tavern. If there is wine, I'm a corridor. In the waking life, this room is dim. So many weeks this year, I have slept alone in beds which are not my own. The doors are numbered 2, 27, 36, 409, 212. An assortment of keys. Here two windows open to the sea saying, You did not go far enough yet.

Your friend says, Everyone in the world is coupled. The universe is Noah's ark and those without a mate will drown. At night, in restaurants, I think of suicide, but in the morning, the poem holds out its hand.

As you would guess, the Inn is haunted. They say the ghost of a woman wanders in the rooms. She hung herself from the rafter, just below the Chinese goddess of evil who breathes the dark. Yet the morning was ferns, blue glass and orchids. Gulls catch the afternoon light. Twice we talked on the phone through the sunset. We are friends also in the odd moments that matter between women.

In Boston, I met a Black poet in exile from his people. He drinks from the same river as women alone. The shadow of the poet carrying the universe is a hunchback. These portraits of myself as stone, while poems lope on all fours.

Yes, we'll visit. You ask me to come in summer when we can sail, but I think it shall always be winter for those who court the weather and like men fierce and knowledgeable about hard things. Still, I urge you to build the May altar. It is not too late for you to wind flowers. You are good in the hands. And even I gather pussy willows from the dune forest where picnic tables were drowning in the lake. Maybe spring is not beyond us, only delayed.

This is called Land's End. The slow tide covers the prints of little feet. Prepare for the underwater sleep. Temporarily I am living in the house of illuminated fish, stumbling alone, arms extended through the phosphorescent dark.

In the night, the embrace of two hands passes for a dream. In the day, I hold a walking stick. You live in another country where I used to know the weather.

Under the sea, the typhoon carries a harp of kelp. The song is lament. Rain can not reach me at a thousand fathoms. I am afraid I will forget to brush my hair. Which waters carry this message to you, and what vial will I find to fit it?

Be alert for sailors, the drone of buoys, and the man who dove into the sea for us and brought up my key. So there must be a door here even in these depths. This morning, my father said, "I am the loneliest man in America," but Bim had nowhere in the universe to receive mail. A long time ago, he taught us shipwreck. In this drowning, can I remember my name?

Provincetown: Jane

My hands in your coat. The skins are small and no
one identifies the smooth and tiny animal. Something
I can not name keeps me warm. I am practicing
loneliness, become a virtuoso. In my old age, I will be
prepared for what I can not bear but will wear like
this old coat, the one you gave me that warm season,
in preparation for winter. Where we live, the snows
do not blow between our fingers.

There is no laughter in the single country, and I
am given cramped rooms. One had no light and two
beds, and here the room lined with books is smaller
than my pen. Outside this room, in wicker chairs
among the ferns and orchids, couples sit in the
afternoon sun of idle conversation against which I
open and close the doors. The room is improvised for
a maiden aunt or other odd creatures. Herons and
cranes could nest here. I have seen the pain braiding
through your straw hair.

This may be the last of my inexplicable solo
voyages. This morning, I thought of all the times we
walked the beach. You would like it here. The dunes
loom like great white breasts on the hides of
elephants. The nipples of thunderous beasts. Why
don't we live in herds? You never travel alone.
Wisdom doesn't protect me, doesn't remind me that
dreams are only night friends. We could breakfast
together in this Inn as the stained glass calls the
light—burgundy, gold, cobalt blue. The gulls say the
wind is to be passed through. I can not pass thorough
my own heart.

Thoreau wrote a book about the Cape and I came here hoping the solitary would find her own shadow on the sand pleasing. Thoreau lived alone and sang about it, but in my wandering, I have found pleasure only where there is absolutely no one at all, not even myself.

Why do I leave home? Because I don't like Sunday company. If I call you tonight, will I learn you made another life? The day before we both left, our carpets covered with neat piles of shoes and sweaters and scarves as if bravery were a knowledge of wools and silks. I am brave, my friend, and look to delight the lonely eye.

Tomorrow where no one speaks, I can have a love affair with gulls. Where are you wandering? Your daughter loved horses and lives at home. That is, a man has never rubbed her body down. We were broken into early. Perhaps I am an empty bowl, one of the old shards so valuable to museums. I do not like afternoon tea though visits are the life I have. Promise not to let me do this again.

On the dunes, I wonder when you will leave home. The snow is falling but does not stick to the ground. Salt from the sea erodes what comes down. When I was a kid, rock salt on the sidewalks against the ice.

A man built this Inn as an aerie and afterwards never ventured out. Though I've tried to build a house of life with my hands, I'm left to be the chronicler of carpenters. Are you leaving just as I call myself, Spinster, and settle down into the smallest possible room?

Provincetown: Holly

The mysteries derive from what must not be told.
The language of gulls is clear, but we must not speak
it even in a dream. The tide covers what the moon
bares. Had we talked, I would have told you the
secret dream which brought me to this pale house of
many colors. The aborigine did not know the origin
of his own child but knew what must not be said.
The imperative of Dream Time is silence. I have been
profligate with my secrets. The sign says, 'Dunes are
fragile.' A few bits of straw hold them in place. Only
the wind's feet can brush across the sand without
doing harm.

In the dream, the city is unknown. Stone buildings
rise up, thin and cramped. The road rises up, dips
straight down, depending on perspective. Where
you've been. Where it's time to go. At my right
shoulder, the young man says, "You've come down
hill. It's time to rise." Gulls sweep effortlessly across
the hill pointing toward these New England moors.
Houses rise in three stories. The young man asks if I
wish to meet the poet whose voice is a stone in the
world. I say, I'd rather study with the sea, am
looking for teachers without voices, have heard the
lyre of the waves in a dark country which has no
public name. Then in the dream, clapboard houses
appear, pale pastel colors, luminous with an inner
light.

In this house, eggs painted with the care of birds.
It's bitter cold. On the way, a snow storm surprised
sparrows thinking of spring, nesting in these northern
trees. I did not ask for solitude, but it is given to me
with my name.

These letters to blond women who wear pale colors and know endurance. The wind is gray. The snow falls white, pales the red roofs. We can not see fire through the chimney. Even in the summer under the wildest bougainvillaea, the twigs are brown. Color an afterthought. In the beginning, there was the earth. You know her by her skin. I am learning the silence of the roof of my mouth. A poet friend tells me city pigeons huddle by chimneys of public buildings during the worst frosts. I have been chasing winter this year as if he were a lover.

We have walked together. I think you know this coast, have dreamed fishermen from Portugal and the gray doom O'Neill unearthed from these dunes. Once I found a beach near our footsteps of rounded glass becoming translucent stones when the sea rushed in. Wandering down the Cape, the Boston Charles wasn't water enough. The man says this is Buffalo grass. What does the beast say about wanderers? Can he read the images painted on his skin? Would I have lived in a luminous house made of his hide?

I want to be where the light persists, spending the day hovering in the white spectrum of light, photographing my shadow. From the image, you will never know if I am one of the dark women or become one of the light. The shadow begins the dream. In the Mysteries, initiates descended into the center of the earth and told—nothing. They said, "She Whose Name I Will Not Say." The dream is like the wind. From this window, I know it only by what it moves.

Nothing is steady under our feet. Even reefs toss in
the sea. I said, I had dismantled my life, had courted
emptiness to see what new would enter. You said,
emptiness follows emptiness. We strip to the bones to
see the bones. You say, we have no wonders coming
to us in our lives.

We have continuity in small things, you and I.
Years now we know each other and gather May,
October hours in bars and restaurants. We have had
five o'clocks for twenty years.

This is the country of widow's walks. You can not
comfort me. I have lost more than I care to name to
the sea and will sing my own pain. It is a woman's
coming of age. You knew her body when she
considered herself a girl. Can we desire each other
again? There is one gift: we age together. Imagine the
opposite: time staggering, erratic like the light on the
reef which has gone out. Someone has shipwrecked
before I will. Someone said, "This is the time."

Do these morsels with friends sustain me? I marvel
that I pursue them. The road map points in one
direction. It is my beauty, these lines on my face. I
have come three thousand miles to eat alone.

The Lutheran said, "Coney Island does not exist. No one comes from there but fools." I didn't get to Steeplechase. Laughter is difficult and Luna Park burned down when we were kids. We never met in our old streets, but when I walk this sand, I remember why you hate the beach. Your summers under the boardwalk, selling umbrellas, trying to stay out of the sun. My Boston friend asks, "Don't you read? You can't go home again." I have been home and home and home. I can not get away. At ten each night, I walk this cape. Old habits. Lighthouse. Salt. Rain. I am walking a maze as a blind man gropes angrily through his garden. But the old woman says, "Chair, you have been under me all these years."

Coming from the sea, which freezes like the gray wood it leeches, how did you dream a gypsy? I say he belongs to me. You say, the dream is a gift, but how can I enter your sleep and claim what is mine?

I look for any sign. Tinker wagons. Stolen horses. Knives. Once I met a gypsy on the wild moor and heard his violin, put coins in his little velvet pouch. But it was long before I learned to love a man with broken teeth.

Are there any tents or goats in this country of grays and browns? Last night, I thought, She has broken me down, broken me down. I have come to the dry point of the meeting of the desert and the sea and do not know where to die of thirst or be delivered. On this lonely path, I was thinking, this is the way He led his followers; but I didn't expect to see Her hand in this.

Valyermo: Robert

I called you Rio, thinking that rivers are always
filling from secret streams and entering the sea so
that they are never dry at the feet and there is
someplace they are always going. Even in their
drying, we call them rain.

I refuse all sacrifices, while you volunteer the
giving up of the heart. In your room, two little beds
and you live alone. Identical blankets covered my bed
when I was a child. My heart is wrenched from me as
rubble is scattered to gulls and nothing comes of it.
Once long ago, I heard you groan, "Need. Need.
Need."

Yet when we talk, it is always about dancing. You
saw the dance of two hands—lovers, separated by a
window, tracing each other's fingers. And the line
dance which says, we must never be set apart. Once
we danced wild and naked as Shiva danced when he
created the world. The gods devour us but not before
our joy. We have shared a dream with bare feet.

I am tired of altars with hearts on them, am wary
of vultures and other dark birds. Where are the
hands to dismantle the stones of loneliness, one by
one? I dreamed the rain dance, but nothing for light.

You had a name for me, something to do with
birds. I can not remember it. Do I come out of this
storm with a leaf in my mouth?

You call suddenly. Full moon fading. Van der Post
said the guards were cruelest—POW Camp World
War II—during the full moon.

Cruel is the address of this house, I say. Lilith, you
say, is the dark moon. I say, She lives here. She has
fallen on me. I say, I am cut down to the bone and
still the laser comes. I am reduced by this pillar of
light called guillotine.

Lilith, you say. I am in her shadow. She turns her
dark hair to the sun to take his light in her eyes. It
seems he turns aside.

You say, Don't take the path of Lilith and her
vengeance against the men who threw her out. But
why is my lot always with the exiled ones? Luna
retreats once a month from His insistent gaze, but He
slips by Lilith every night.

Lilith. Darkness turning. We mark her movements
by the great hole in the sky. Eve, Eve, I am even more
willing than you to lie down under his nuclear light.
Some walk the dark side, but I will cross the fire
barefooted. Victor, remember Van Gogh in his
madness in Arles shouting, 'The light, the light!'

Valyermo: Judith

On both sides, your people have trickster gods. The first night here, coyotes under my floor.

I never thought to ask: does a returning bird ever nest alone? If there can be no eggs, can there be no home? Every tree married to the earth.

Alone in the night, I see the moon, bare assed and laughing.

WALKING WITH NERUDA

In 1988, I imagined a relationship with Pablo
Neruda. This is the record of that friendship.

Pablo Neruda, I introduce myself as the one who is behind you. I sleep under your feet and walk where you walked. Perhaps I walked to Chile, for since I learned your name, I could do nothing but walk after you. After I read your poems, I walked in my sleep.

In Chile, I pursued you. When you took walks, I followed you to know how a poet walks. When you walked with your wife, I followed the two of you. I noticed when you stopped, when you spoke to each other, when you were silent. I had to learn from the tone of your back when you were looking inward, when you were looking out. I was determined to know how you turned what you came upon into words.

I followed you for weeks. You allowed me the dignity of being unacknowledged. I fell in beside you after I had followed you day after day in the rain. Did you love the world so much that bitter cold and wind could not dissuade you from pursuing it?

I began to believe that I would learn everything if I watched you walk, even if I never had read a single poem you wrote, or never looked into your face. I began to believe that you were your back, the sound of your feet, the route you chose. You were no more—but no less—than your consistent deliberate habit of walking. You were your feet despite anything and everything that might still happen or had already happened. You were your feet, despite the newspaper headlines, visiting dignitaries, urgent telephone calls, coups, persecutions and all siren songs.

One day when your feet became the universe itself,
I fell in alongside you. You didn't speak; you were
always the poet. Once, I tripped and you put out
your hand to steady me, but this also without a
word. And once—before we had spoken a word—
you tipped your hat, a trifle mischievously, I thought,
as you went into the house. After a while, I liked to
think you were waiting for me each day, that you
hesitated just a moment at the door, looking about
without looking, before you set out for the sea.

I wanted to be your lover, your sister and your
shadow. I wanted to be the paper you wrote upon
and the air you breathed. I wanted to know
everything without interfering or deflecting you in the
slightest from the splendid and eloquent isolation of
your stride. If I could, I would have been the road
extending myself in rock and sand to the print of
your feet, rolling endlessly under you.

Finally, I spoke. You said, "Don't speak. Not
here. Not now. Coffee is for speaking, also
aguardiente. Speech is best at five in the afternoon
with a little brandy. Also it is good to speak after ten
at night, after a rich *sopa de mariscos* and over an
extraordinary Chilean *vin ordinaire*. But in the rain
and fog while walking, it is best to be silent. Here the
poem is born into words only if nothing is said."

I listened. I nodded to indicate I'd understood
what you said. You saw my hunger. You passed a
few dry twigs to me, some yellow and orange leaves,
the black stones of Isla Negra. At the knees of the
sea, you bent down, straining your portly body, to
dip your fingers into the foam and press the salt
water to my lips. It occurred to me to eat everything

you gave me, even soil, to ingest the elements of earth from which you made a poem. I began to understand the terrifying and necessary intimacy with the world which poetry requires.

When you felt that I was becoming deeply acquainted with the silence, when you saw that I was no longer speaking words in my head, when you saw that I could forget words altogether for miles at a time, you invited me into your house.

Bienvenido.

I had imagined conversation. Surely, he was one of the great talkers. I thought I needed that talk. After all, I came to him frightened, a dumb teenage girl with shaking hands, essentially insecure about language. Moses, who is in my lineage, put coals in his mouth and stuttered afterwards, while I imagined that doves flew out of Pablo's mouth whenever he spoke. *Palomas. Palomas blancas* quivering wings. Words like startled feathers. *Un nido* of burning sentences.

I imagined long literary evenings, odes intoned to the beat of the *charanga*, gossip long as gallows, speeches pregnant with clouds and grammatic shadows. *La noche escondida, la mascara* of painted *palabras*, lucid *pajaros de la anochecida.*

He gave me a blank piece of paper. "Dare," he laughed.

When I entered his day room, whirring white doves, their eyes *brillantes entre dos luces de cobre,* settled into their golden cages. I called to them, "Coo, coo," and my breath smudged the night with coal dust, *negra y pesada.*

If I write this, if I dare to imagine the moment—as I have imagined others—where a man or a woman who had no prior existence suddenly grow ruddy with the breath of life on the page—if I dare to imagine this: myself, this poet named Pablo Neruda, the two of us together in a room—*viviendonos*—he hasn't died yet—poetry is still possible—it is raining in the south of Chile.... I know the landscape. *La lluvia* of hope...

A woman who writes a word down is not the same as the one who does not.

When I was not yet twenty-four, I followed Pablo Neruda, the world's greatest poet, into his house.

He said, "A woman rarely becomes a poet because the fathers tell her to keep her body closed and the mothers agree. If you want to write, you will have to be as open as the sea. *Apertura lluviosa.*" He said, "Live in my house for a month and don't speak. *Mi casa es tu casa-miento incomunicado.*"

I wanted to have a poem and I was pregnant. I was
very thin. As if I'd lived on air. A poet must be able
to live on air, but a mother must not attempt it. My
mother wanted me to buy a set of matching pots,
Wearever aluminum, like the ones she had. They
were heavy and had well fitting lids so my suppers
wouldn't burn. My husband wanted me to give
dinner parties. John F. Kennedy was running for
office.

I sensed danger. Kennedy wasn't against the Bomb
or for nuclear disarmament. I joined SANE at its
inception. Also Concerned Scientists. I spoke with
Linus Pauling and encouraged my husband to help
his partner organize Physicians for Social
Responsibility.

There was a baby in my belly. I wanted to write
poems. I had a crazy idea that a woman could write a
real novel, the kind that shook the world. I
hallucinated that a woman could be a poet, but she
would have to be free. And I couldn't imagine that
freedom for myself even though I could see it in Isla
Negra when I followed Pablo Neruda. I could see it
in the way he walked. Even if he were walking inside
a dictatorship, among guns, soldiers and spies, there
was nothing between him and his vision. Anything he
saw, he was able to take into himself—there was no
sight, no image, no vision to which he didn't feel
entitled. In his heart, everything—everything—
belonged to him. Pablo Neruda was—more than
anything—a poet, and so he was an entitled man.

I was a woman and entitled to nothing. I had nothing except a husband, a rented house, a set of pots, living room furniture, a frenzy of obligations, credit cards, anxious relatives, too many acquaintances, a gift of future diaper service, two telephones, no time to read, a plastic wrapped cookbook of recipes gleaned from the pages of the New York Times, and a hunger, a terrible hunger for the unimaginable, unlimited freedom of being a poet and a baby in my belly.

I would have called Pablo long distance if I had the courage, if I had the ability to speak Spanish fluently, if we had ever talked about real things. But, what would a man know about a baby in the belly? And what did it matter if there were to be one poet more or less in the world when so many in his country were dying?

I woke up one morning and thought—I can't have this child. My husband said, "You'll have to get a job after it's born so we can buy a house. You'll need an advanced degree so you can do something." I thought, I can't. I have to write a poem. My mother found a crib. Someone painted it white. A friend sent a pastel mobile with tame wood animals. I thought about blue curtains, making bedspreads and abortions.

Pablo was silent. He was walking so far away from me, I couldn't hear him. My husband objected to donating more free medical care to the Black Panthers. I tried to make dolmades from scratch and located grape leaves preserved in brine at the Boys' market twenty miles away. I organized a write-in campaign against JFK. My husband thought it would be nice to have teatime with the children and romantic dinners by ourselves. The new formula bottles lined up on the sink like tiny bombs. The U.S. was pursuing overground testing; I was afraid the radiation would cross the milk barrier. I had a poem in me howling for real life but no language to write in. The fog came in thick, flapping about my feet like blankets unraveling. I became afraid to have a daughter.

I called Pablo Neruda in the middle of the night as he walked underwater by Isla Negra. He moved like a dream porpoise. He seemed pregnant with words. They came out of his penis in long miraculous strings. The sea creatures quivered with joy. I said, "Pablo, I want to know how to bear the child in my belly onto this bed of uranium and I want to know if a woman can be a poet." He was large as a whale. He drank the sea and spouted it in glistening odes, black and shiny. I said, "I can't have this child," and he laughed as if he had never done anything but carry and birth children.

So I packed my little bag as if I were going to the hospital and I left a note and the Wearever pots and the sterilized nipples upon the glass missiles, and took the cradle board which an American Indian friend had given me for the baby and which had made my husband snort—"You're not going to carry the thing on your back, are you?" I took some money, the car, some books, paper and pens, my walking shoes, an unwieldy IBM electric typewriter, my pregnant belly and a dozen cloth diapers, and I went out.

I knew how to carry a baby and how to carry a poem and would learn how to have a baby and even how to have a poem. I would have enough milk for both, and I would learn how to walk with them. But I didn't know, and didn't want to know, how to have a husband and a matched set of Wearever pots.

Pablo Neruda's cheeks arc along his jowls like the folds of old cloth. His stomach is immense. *San Pablo. San Pablo de las palabras.* I dream I am lovers with this great ugly man, am sleeping at sea level beneath the mountain of his belly, lying down on a bed of worn drawers and linen undershirts. San Pablo is the range of great hills from Chillán to Tierra del Fuego. He is the bald earth under the knife of the ice pack, the pumice fist about the fire cone of the volcano.

San Pablo Neruda wears underwear. His robe is frayed. The heavy rope belt with tassels woven of silk threads like the one my father wore the year that I was born rings the bells, *él pica la campana, él da una campanada de poesia.*

Pablo Neruda wears knit wool socks, a sailor's cap, and rough pants with copper buttons on the fly. His mouth bears the wide gash of a smile like the blasted entrance to Santa Maria de Iquique. His eyes have the scratch of salt. Grit of pepper under his nails, yeast smoking in his voice, skin soft as the oldest *paño de cocina.* The earth is rising in him, *como un horno de fuego* smoldering in the high desert. Bread man, pot holder, *panza* of the Sierras, take me into the steaming loaf.

Exploring With Neruda

I come to Neruda the way I had pursued the great explorers when I was a child. Magellan, De Soto, Amundsen, Pizarro, Balboa compelled me with a bitter attraction. Because I am a woman, I knew that I would never be prepared for their adventures. I could never man the ship to find the undiscovered waterway, the unknown continent. But, there are ways, I insisted, through which even a woman can explore the world. I imagined an inner landscape and craved the volcanos and high seas of the imagination. These, I believed, would display themselves to me when I found a guide to lead me to the moist stony passages between the worlds.

Neruda knew the way across. I came to Chile to follow him through an arch of granite opened by the beating of the gray turbulent sea, *el pacifico del invierno.*

When I was a very young girl, I walked the quiet blocks of my neighborhood, rounding the circle between the ocean and the bay, circling from the abandoned hospital ship, across the deserted marshes to the jetties on the farthest beaches. When I wondered why I was compelled to take this walk each night, I told myself, I am practicing to be a poet—a poet is someone who knows how to walk.

I liked the mist, the foam and spray, salt and the slippery rocks, sand—pale as dawn—seaweed, crustaceans, silver fish, geysers and whirling undulations, mud and the obscured moon, red tides and sunrises boiling out of the sea. These were the cognates of my mind, the rise and fall, the approach and the recession, the appearance and disappearance of what I knew and did not know.

Pablo Neruda knew this territory and I came to him, not to hear his poems, nor gather his wisdom, but to follow him when he was lost, to accompany him when he was drowning, and to listen whenever he was mute. He was my Henry Hudson, the Vasco da Gama of my childhood faith. I had practiced long enough alone to want a teacher. So I followed Pablo Neruda down under the sea *a sondar* the continent of my own silence among the precipitous fathoms of the *desconocido*.

Pablo Speaks About the Girl

Once an unknown boy passed a toy sheep through a hole in a fence and I instantly became a poet. Ever since, I have been moved by the appearance of small hands, have treasured gifts and holes in fences. I walk into the fog because I never know what will be revealed when it opens its mouth. I walk into the mouth of fog as into the mouth of the shark. What is given to us, what we take, devours us. In a moment—chomp—we are holy mincemeat in the teeth of the gift.

She had small nervous hands as if what she gave she wanted to snatch away immediately. What if that little boy had been ashamed of his gift? Had thought it too small or too worn? There in the poverty of his embarrassment, a poet would have died. Don't you see, it was his clarity, his confident and unselfconscious generosity which transformed me irrevocably—for better or worse—into the man I am.

I've been stalked before, usually by madwomen and hungry men who want to savor a bit of a poet on the installment plan. They nibble at me cautiously as if they can take a taste on consignment. If it is too bitter—spit it out.

She was neither mad nor hungry. She was painfully shy and completely unsure of herself. She could hardly speak Spanish and at times I thought English was equally difficult for her. Immediately, I knew she had the destiny to be a poet, she was so unsure of words.

I let her follow me. So respectful of my distance, she was like the wind asking permission before inserting itself in the tree. Moments after she appeared, I forgot her, as the moving branch forgets movement, but then I remembered when her silent presence alerted me to myself. So, the branch finally knows its own stillness through its trembling. She was unsure of herself in all ways except in her intractable, unshakable curiosity, except in the clarity of her confident and unselfconscious right to know; so, finally, her curiosity determined mine.

For a girl to dare this... Correction, you say, at twenty-four a girl is a woman. A girl, I tell you, politics be damned, she was a girl, *una niña, nada mas,* for a girl to dare this....

I wondered what she would write eventually. Oh, not about me. Such a piece, whatever it might be, would be banal. A poet—even a great poet—is only that. No more interesting than a seal bellying onto a rock. What would she say when she saw what she had come to see? I went inside myself to seek that vision for her as conscientiously as I had explored each fence hole for a secret hand.

My country was on the brink of internal war. Everything I believed in—no!—nothing I believed in, but everything I had hoped for—was about to be shattered like a wave smashed to foam against a cliff. I was old and sick—who wouldn't be?—and behind me—protecting my back from the assassin's knife of hopelessness and despair—was a girl who still believed—hoped—there was something to know.

I never walked as carefully as I did during those months when I went first and she followed. In reality, she led with her curiosity and I followed with mine as steadfastly as a gull follows a fish. I wanted to give her everything that had once mattered—the fog, the cormorants, the stones, the wet and acid earth, sand, seaweed, red tide—I gave them all to her. Soon the generals would come for everything which remained and I would die. Then afterwards a girl with shaking hands might have the will to shape salty mud into a world again.

Pablo speaks:

Yo sueño en color, I dream in color, and awaken
to the gray wave, edged white foam, playing itself
free of the black sea. Gulls with bleached feathers
streak across the platinum disk of the sun. My hands
lose their ruddiness in the fog. I anticipate a poor
meal of porridge and black olives. Someone has
nicked the arteries of my country and it has gone
pale; the blood of the people coagulates on the gray
pavement like a black scab.

She is waiting for me in her red sweater with furry
balls on both sides of her head. "Earmuffs," she
whispers to me, knowing I enjoy English. The
earmuffs are red. Also her nose. And her cheeks.

It will be gray in Chile this season when the spirit
fades in the relentless cold and poverty steals the
blues and yellows, the ochers, greens and magentas
from the eyes and heart. Or will it be fear? Or will it
be despair?

In Santiago, along the Rio Mapocho, the Ramona
Parra Brigada painted a long mural of stars, doves,
and fists in brilliant, preposterous, primary colors
now drowning in whitewash and lies. When I
remember how it was, I think of all the inmates who
spend their days painting the grass green. I would,
myself, paint the sky blue, if I did not know that
skies fall down in the black night.

I was grateful for her sweater and called to her to
take my hand. It was not for love, but for the hope of
the touch of the fiery red wool cuff against my wrist.

I have been given only one task in this life: not to fall into despair, and I have failed it. At least once, I want to write something so simple, so ordinary and so familiar: 'ruby lips, eyes blue as cornflowers, hair *muy negro*, porcelain hands...' This is not how she looks, but these commonplaces reassure me that color once existed and that I am not alone.

I asked her to model for me, to walk fast without looking back, to run without glancing over her shoulder, to leap without fear from one boulder to another. A painter might have asked her to sit without moving, but I needed the reassurance of her stride and the free song from her mouth, the pink of her tongue clanging against the rosy roof of her mouth. I wanted to see the opals of her breath in the ice crystals of frost. I had to believe that something can be alive.

Red light. Green light. *Rojo. Verde. Amarillo. Purpura. Naranja. Azul. Verde. Rojo.*

Yes, take off your clothes. Yes, I would like to see your hips move. Yes, to see your nipples redden when I pinch them.

The footprint of the soldier is always gray; it presses the color out of everything. Life freezes about the police. They bear down and we are buried under a relentless and merciless glacier.

I said nothing of this to her. I said, "Let's get a cup of tea. Tell me about your life." She was trembling. "New life," I thought, dreaming of tremulous butterflies, wet and brilliant, emerging from chrysali.

I wondered if I would love my country so much if it were not endangered. Frailty in others is an occasion for hope in oneself. The embrace is the central activity of the sea, it slides continually in erotic agitation over the limbs of the creatures it loves.

I was glad she was a woman not a child. She had a womb within her, and I was dreaming its rosy contours, its silky iridescence, its internal moire patterns, soft and pristine. She wanted to be a poet and I was secretly betraying her, even if I wasn't planning a seduction, because I was trying to save myself by planting the seed of my imagination in her womb.

The police were going to come wanting to burn all my work. The white papers still wet with black ink were threatened with foul smoke and boot prints. The air was thick with a noxious gray miasma of a lifetime come to naught. But what I might plant in her womb could grow like a secret code coming to life, a mysterious apparition, a desperate immaculate conception.

She had blood in her. She had rosy cheeks. Her lips were like rubies. Her lips were like garnets. Copper cheeks, eyes of lapis lazuli. Tongue red as an adder, fingers like salamanders, nipples like burning coals, labia sweet as peonies, anus tight as raspberries, clit like a cardinal, womb of the fire bird.

I betrayed her in the cafe. I wanted to make a child with her. I wanted to tell her I would die in September on the 23rd, but, if she agreed, we could have a child by the following June. She was chatting away. She was stumbling through a morass of Spanish, picking up one word then another, in no order whatsoever, but that of chance and delight. I looked at her longingly and ordered another *aguardiente*. Then I reached for her hand and told her...nothing. "Nothing is more sacred than the life of a poem. It must be carried to term; it must never be aborted."

I saw your funeral on American t.v. It was a double
death. The media took away what was already gone.
After a few minutes, the picture shifted to Vietnam
and you were erased.

I collect artifacts of the dead. The wing of an owl,
the thigh bone of an elk, the heel of a buffalo, an
abandoned nest sit on my altar. I would like to have,
as a talisman, the three fingers which held your pen.

The last time we were together is eclipsed, like the
smoke of a burning city eclipses the sun, by your
death. Better that cancer had really taken you—the
unnatural ravishing of the body—its peculiar and
unfathomable decay as one cell after another turns
against itself—than that you died of heartbreak in the
middle of your own deathbed.

The last time we were together, I hoped the press
of your fingers would imprint poetry upon me while I
wondered how much terror I had to drink to write a
poem. I felt a peculiar and unwelcome feminine
reluctance to invite the world into my body.

I wanted to be one of your heirs. I wanted you to
put your hand on my head the way Jacob blessed his
sons and would have gladly cheated you the way
Jacob cheated Isaac into blessing him. I did not want
an exclusive but a portion of a birthright. I wanted to
know if you could imagine a woman continuing your
line. Did it occur to you that a woman could carry
galaxies within her womb? Do you believe the heart
of a woman is large enough to carry a planet, even a
country, and still small enough to embrace a man
and a child?

I loved you, Pablo Neruda, not the way a woman loves a man, but the way your feet loved soil, the way the moon loves death, the way you walked about Isla Negra in the rags of fog, the way the sun hankers for the green rush in all living things, and the way the mouth hungers for a word. And I still love you, Pablo Neruda, and want to snatch the white bird song from your beak as you streak across the white sky, in your white plumage cawing at the bird of death.

The phone rang at 7 a.m. this morning. After a long silence, a very young boy said, "Die." The world shattered as it had last Sunday when I walked through the arcade behind the young toughs lined up at the slot machines, punk kids jacking off in unison at electric urinals. Across from them, a young *Latina* mother held her baby up to a mounted machine gun and pressed his hands on the trigger, the barrel pointing at an elusive but animated enemy in a cardboard, tropical jungle, called *America del Sur*. *El muerto* is alive and well in *el mundo*.

Later I walked on the beach past the tents of the homeless huddled together in the diminishing area allowed to the squatters. A woman had used four small sticks to designate her territory, claiming a square irregular as a carton which had been squashed. Emblazoned with four red scraps of cloth, these *palos* reserved three feet by four feet of sand. Inside she had firmly planted a red shoe with a cuban heel next to a small pillow and a plastic fork.

A small boy passes the woolly lamb of his need through the tangle of phone wires. There are fences everywhere. Small hands pass furtive messages through whatever holes exist. I followed you for weeks from *hoya a hoya*, even to your grave.

Anything which is passed through the hole in the fence can be a gift. I hung up too quickly on the young boy. He needed a mother at the end of the anonymous phone line to ask him if he'd had his breakfast yet or whether he had brushed his teeth. I could have said, "*Hijo*, thank you for calling, but you'll be late for school." I could have taken his address to send him a woolly lamb with four worn wooden wheels.

Sometimes I forget you, Pablo Neruda. Sometimes I am unable to believe in our friendship. Sometimes I do not believe I have the right to my own audacity. But other times, without warning or permission, you grow in me again. This pregnancy waxes and wanes like the moon. My lunar longing for the word, for the light, *alumbramiento*.

In this moment, wanting to claim my rights, I stop to breathe, as we used to pause when we walked together among *las piedras de Isla Negra*. A contraction rises like a mountain and falls into the sea, and a current takes me, or an eddy of wind bears me up as I bear down.

I look about me into a room of air and fog, filled with spray, gray as cold dusk, *tremoloso* with the last calls of the seagulls before the dark *anochecida, el grito* of sand, walls carved from incontrovertible rock. I shiver from the cold and press myself against the bulk of a walrus of a man whom I pursue from one hemisphere to another. I feel a raft of ice break off within me. The season changes. A warmer current insists itself. And something is born in *el aire libre*, out of the air.

She asks permission to be a poet: *Con su permiso,
Señor, por favor, Señor, Excuseme, Señor,
autorizeme, Señor déme poder á...* Señor. Though
she pursued me to Chile, she does not know she has
the right to poems, that words can belong to her.

This is not a literary issue. This is a political issue;
it is not about entitlement. Titles, we explain to the
workers, are often abrogated, ownership can be
challenged. Land which properly belongs to peasants
is too often appropriated by landlords, armies and
governments. But there are rights which are prior to
law, power or territory. These include her right to the
word. *Derecho.*

When she thinks in terms of rights, entitlements
and empowerment, she is thinking with men's words.
So, she argues with herself. She is alternately judge,
lawyer, accuser and defendant. She argues her right
to be a poet, and then she abdicates her right to a
series of phone calls, the demands of the checkbook,
friendships, maternal obligations, the accounting of
small personal needs. She approaches this issue as if
it fell within the purview of civilization, within
divisions of time, systems of priorities, hierarchies of
values, checks, and balances, duties and obligations,
work and leisure, needs and satisfactions, gifts and
reciprocities.

How do you tell a woman to respect nature
without insulting her?

You must take her by the hand. You must walk
long enough for walking to become instinct, for the
wolf born in captivity to be wild, for *la loba* to find
the wild thing.

I am a poet so I bring her seawater, a grain of
sand, grief as heavy as my body to hold in her hands.
The water dries to salt. She doesn't remember. She
must take herself by her hand. I am a dead man.
How can the dead teach the living about real things?

I want to tell her: A poet is a fact of nature, is
relentless as *la borrasca*, as absolute as drought,
intractable as lava, inexorable as *el temblor*, as
insistent as *las tormentas*. Storm wants neither
permission nor privilege. A poet doesn't ask, doesn't
argue or cajole. A poet is a revolution, *crece salvaje*.
She was born to the wrong mother. Had a wolf
raised her, she would be writing songs to break *el
corazon de la montaña*.

My words, *mis palabras*, were intended to bring the
suffering in the world into myself, for the desperate
and passionate lives of men to live within me. I didn't
want to be immune to or ignorant of any
particularity. The humble ones, *los humildes*, the
ones without clothes, *los pobres*, especially, I didn't
want to live without their sores and orgasms
enlivening, *viviendo*, in my own body. I wanted to
know all life and by my death, to know everyone's
death. My death, then, in particular, the last to be
known.

I used words singular as terror, indelible as a scar
to engrave the exact qualities of another's life upon
me. Like Kafka, I made the word an instrument,
writing, deeper and deeper into my flesh, the name of
human suffering. Also joy. *El alegria*. That too, by
necessity, as painful. When I was breaking under the
pain and ecstasy of it, that was the redemption. The
isolation broken. The secret of skin displayed in
banners, bandannas, *banderolas, vendajes y
bandidos*. The flag of my life, the determined
weather, marking the wind, forever.

I was a great whale in a black sea. When I spouted, the white water sprayed onto the waves in burning letters. All of history burned into the sea through this alphabet. But I was a whale and understood none of it. The water which flooded into me was all my knowledge and also all my ignorance. So it went on for eons. The black sea, viscous and inky, was seared by the incomprehensible script of white lightning erupting from the top of my head.

Sometimes I wished I were blind to the light of these mysterious words and longed to navigate by sound like other whales, but I also knew that the letters of fire shook the depths in thunderous crackling swells.

Still, I dove deep hoping to stifle the burning insistence of these words under tons of water, but breath—*la necesidad*—pulled me out from under the subaquatic tremors. Finally, exhausted, I closed my beady whale eyes and let myself float like dead weight to the beach.

The salt dried on me. I could feel my whale spirit contract like a dead skin. The sun attacked me, but its lethal heat was a relief from the demand of the fiery words. I gave myself over gladly to the mute arms of death, sighing.

My breath went out of me. I refused to pull it in. Then salt water flooded my throat. Startled, I blew it out and opened my outraged eyes. Even here on the beach, water fell on me like stars. The sand was full of words. Each grain insisted its own truth. They flew about me like comets.

I saw a young woman opening my mouth and pouring salt water into it from a transparent bucket. She was running to the sea, filling the bucket with flames and pouring them into me. When I spouted, she caught the words in a trough she made out of her skirt and placed them neatly on a black scroll she'd laid out on the sand.

"These are very nice," she said. "They will do. They're really quite enough, you know, for a beginning. We will get quite far with these. We've never seen anything like it."

I wanted to ask her what she meant, but I had no words of my own and was quite parched while she was arranging the shimmering syllables on her scroll.

"You've worked hard," she said. "Would you like a bath?" and pointed me back to the sea which had turned magenta.

The scroll became two large columns, as if from a broken temple, and between them the pole of my body, like a waterfall, rising and falling. Out of respect, I put on a dark suit and a red tie and my blue cap, of course. She took my arm and we went to the shore for the solitude of it.

The ocean roiled in winter flames. She took a glass of wine from her pocket and a gardenia before she placed me on the palm of her hand. I was frail as a minnow.

"So, I am safe at last," I whispered, liking gills a great deal and hoping she was pleased by my iridescence. Her hair was long as seaweed, and she was crying soundlessly. I was so small, she let me swim in the glass bowl of her belly.

"We're never safe," she said. "We don't ever want to be," and she took my hand, and we walked under the sea.

El mar opened like a road, *un camino de posibilidad*, a bridge of *ballenas*, a body celestial and cerulean. We walked into that marriage of water as the heavens descended over us in a riptide of language and pulled us under to all the angels aflame in *la s aguas del poesia* forever.

Naming Us By Our Eyes

A Remembrance of Charlie Chaplin for Ariel

In the beginning we walk on the beach or it is raining
or both and the mist may be the spray of the ocean
but it is the end of a drought and I am grateful for
the rain like the time it was raining in Santiago when
we met. And what we are trying to accomplish now
is a sunburst and you stand at the water's edge and I
walk toward you across the sand and a man stops
me. He says, "The sun hasn't come out though I
prayed for it." "Don't pray now," I beg him, "it's
after sunset. I've had enough miracles today." You're
on the beach and we're together and the drought is
over and last night your plane was late twelve hours
but the CIA didn't get you and you said you had no
trouble with immigration and you're here and the sea
hovers about us and that is miracle enough. And the
man says, "It doesn't matter." He'll pray tomorrow.
"There's a sun," he says. He knows that for sure.
He's seen it though not since you've come. He says
he swears it exists. He knows that for a fact.

In the beginning we walk on the California beach
and you say it is your ocean like the one in Chile, a
little wild and gray and powerful. And you say you'll
take me there when the Junta's dead and we think
next year is a good year, even this year. We're ready.
And we look at the sea and I think it's not only
where we're coming from but where we're going.

I put my feet in the water and know that something of me will eventually be carried down to Chile and we can send messages in bottles to those who have remained there. The fish will transport what we wish. The Junta can not defeat what the ocean carries though they would pass a law against the sea knowing that it holds us. Ultimately they are defeated in every corner. I look at the sea wondering if it is a woman. *La Mer.* Or a man. *El Mar.* Or is it one of those new androgynous creatures we aspire to be? Man and woman in our hearts. We walk on the beach and you say "Someday we will all be entirely woman." But in your poem you said entirely human. *Enteramente humanos.* I think we will all be entirely each other and then we will be ourselves. The ocean leaps toward us with its undefeatable arms.

We are walking the beach, the sun has fallen behind the rain into the sea and steams the air sweet with fish. The ocean escapes toward the sky. We smell its breath. We have taken the job we love of naming and I think it is a way of returning to paradise, this job of counting, of knowing who belongs to us. Everyone who is dear is named. It's how we keep alive, raising a quiet army against those who think they own the sky. I want you to know the best of us. The ones who can look you in the eye and with the ocean as ally. I think even the man who prayed for the sun is eligible. We are few but we are also many and you can name us by our eyes.

And in the beginning as we are walking on the beach, you find a new friend to whom you said in the night, "I'd like to see you again but it's not possible" and he answered, "Don't worry I'll find you." And now he's found you and we're on the beach together and you look each other in the eyes and we walk together by this sea which you say is like your ocean and by the sea where I am always walking when I am naming. And it's dark now and the sun has fallen so far down behind the ocean that even if we stood on each other's shoulders and on tiptoe on the pier we wouldn't be able to see it.

Still your son begins to draw on the dark sand. And he draws a picture of Charlie Chaplin and we laugh at the turned out feet and the round eyes and he draws a big bubble which says *"Je suis Charlie Chaplin."* This is a few hours before we hear that Chaplin has died but we don't know he's dead we're just walking along the beach meeting a friend who said he'd find you and your son's drawing a man with round eyes. And this is the same beach that Charlie walked on and we remember Charlie and we laugh and you laugh because you can't forget anything and you recognize those round brown eyes because you never close your eyes to anything, not even the moment when I hurt you when you said, "We have already had so much if we didn't see each other again it would be enough" and I said, "Yes you're right but still it wouldn't be enough." And I hurt you. For you it has to be enough. It always has to be enough in the moment as it has to be enough for Charlie to have a pair of torn pants and a violin.

You're as homeless as he is and your country's under the fist of Charlie's bully and so you make a violin of poems and play on the streetcorners when you must.

But I'm greedy and also privileged to be able to want more and I want another day and consider asking the man who was praying to bring up the sun to give us another hour but I am afraid of another miracle. And I am thinking as I look at Charlie that I hope I will always have round open little brown eyes like Charlie's and I hope that I will always remember this moment, and I hope I will remember laughter that I will always ... that it will be enough.... And this is the moment they say that Charlie died and we don't know it and so we don't bury him. We are simply noting his presence with us as he catches our eye.

And in the beginning we are walking on the beach and perhaps we are always walking on the beach until you will fly to Chicago. *Chi*-cago you say. *Chi* like the energy which the Chinese see and which we don't. We are walking on the beach and you are telling me about a woman who was healed by a bicycle. The bicycle of the revolution. You say the revolution is a shaman that the revolution can heal even cancer. She's a student in your class and you healed her with a story about a bicycle as you healed my shoulder with just the slightest touch as you looked in my friend's eyes and knew he was a healer. He has it in his hands as you do as we all must carry it in our eyes and hands because that way it's safe and no one can take it from us. No more than they can take the sea from us or the fact that we can see the sun at the same time from different continents and in that moment at eight in the morning and four in the afternoon we can see the sun as mirror and find each other in the reflection. They can't hold us apart though they think they can control our countries. You tell me the story of the healed woman who said, "You bicycled for my life like the cyclist in Antonio Skarmeta's story who bicycled for his mother's life and fought death as he pumped his bicycle his heart breaking up to the top of the mountain. And his mother lived." And you shared that story with the dying woman and told me Tonio had written it and I remember Tonio and how we looked into each other's eyes the last time we met. Everyone had given up the dying woman as everyone too often gives up dying women but you said "No No No. It's a lie. Death is a lie. Don't believe them. Believe you'll live." Pedaling. Pedaling. The heart pumping. And you won.

And we're walking on the beach knowing that we don't quite have the revolution here to pedal for us yet. But we meet these friends on the beach who say they'll find us. And they do. And that's a beginning. And all the sets of eyes we found. And you are pedaling for us and we are pedaling for you. And when I was in Cuba there was a poster of Charlie Chaplin on a bicycle and he was pedaling, he was pedaling for *cinema movil*. They were taking the movies to the countryside to show them to peasants who had never seen movies in their lives and they were carrying the movies on big trucks which they set up in the fields at night under the stars and they took Charlie with them. He was pedaling for them. For the revolution.

You were flying to Chi-cago and we were in the airport elevator and an American man said "We're all going to the same place" and you were thinking "No we're not." And I had your bag on my shoulder and a black beret on my head and I was thinking that I looked like Tania the guerilla. She is dead. But my friend says I look like her and also says I look like Ethel Rosenberg. When he feels loving it is what he says. But Ethel is dead. And they say Charlie is dead. And we're not all going to the same place. And you said the year was full of death for you. It was the year that supposed friends turned against you. And the year was close to death for me. And you said you'll never have a community again until you're home in Chile. But since I didn't die, I said, "My house is your house. *Mi casa es tu casa.*" And you invited my friends in for dinner. And we came in one day from the airport and you said, "We're home." And so we were. And if we never see the house again together it is enough because you're home in it. And that can't end anymore than the sea can end or our eyes can end or the day we met in Santiago, Chile, and it was raining but the sun broke through suddenly and astonished our eyes.

And I say, look at Charlie. He never said 'never.' And he was always playing the violin and crying as you were reading poems to me and crying and I went to the movies when you were gone and saw *1900* and cried and then I thought of Charlie who never said, never, who never learned, never. His gift to us. That he would be kicked out into the street. Beaten up.

Robbed. Betrayed. Almost murdered and he always pedaled back always jumped back up bumped up like those foolish pop-up clowns which you can knock down but they pop-up which can't be defeated if there's air in them. That is, if you've filled them with breath. Didn't you see Charlie pop-up on the beach? Did you think it was a gull? No. You took off your glasses and rubbed your eyes and looked at the sand with your glasses off seeing what your young son had outlined on the brown damp sand. *Je suis Charlie Chaplin. Yo soy Charlie Chaplin.* I am...I am...I am....

We're on the beach and it's barely raining but enough to know the drought is over and we're telling all the stories about all the ones we know. We are a few, so precious, so few I can count us on the fingers of my hand, but then I remember someone else and we are more and we name everyone we know in common, all the Chileans, and all the North Americans, and all the Latinos, and a few Europeans. We name all those we know in common because we're common people and we see eye to eye on this and we run out of fingers and go on to the next hand and run over all our fingers again counting as if we were tying knots in a string adding a knot for each one of us.

I remember the Huichol Indian ceremony where a knot is tied into a string for each one of those who becomes part of the community. A knot for those who go forth and a knot for those who stay behind to tend the fire. And I tie a knot in a string for you for the day when you go forth again and a knot in a string for me because I'll keep the fire. And when the hunt is over they untie themselves from the strings. That is what the Huicholes do. Our *quipo* strings are thick with knots as we talk. Inca counting systems. Storehouses full of grain. I believe it is a time of plenty. We have the seeds hidden and waiting. We count the names on our fingers one knot per name. We will plant the grain soon. In the meantime we keep the seeds between us. When you are a Huichol and you tie yourself into the string, you must confess everything. We tell each other everything we know.

Knotting. A sailor habit. We are by the sea. Soon we will sail back to Chile again. We are telling stories. The ocean comes up to us but it does not erase Charlie Chaplin. The breeze freshens as if to fill the sails which will carry us but the blowing sands do not cover Charlie Chaplin. We walk to the pier to look for the sun and find it gone and the merry-go-round is closed and you call your friends and they aren't home and then they are. The knots get thicker, heavier, fuller. There is more grain in the granary than we know. The *quipo* tell us it will last a long time. When the hunt is over we will not need to untie the knots. Those who tie in with us remain with us. When we met we became tied to each other. I didn't know why then. It was something about keeping our eyes open to each other. It was something about looking at each other in the eyes. It was something about Charlie Chaplin.

When we come home from walking on the beach there is a false news report. Even *The Times* can lie. I hear it repeated on the radio but the best sources can be in error. After all weren't we on the beach at the time of his alleged death which means at that same moment we could have been looking at the sun together if it weren't raining. They say he died in Europe but how could that be? Didn't we see him smiling one foot angling toward the sunrise and one foot angling toward the sunset and an umbrella in his hand because of course it was raining. Before you came there had been a two-year drought and didn't we meet friends whom you thought you would never see again but one of them said quite casually the night before when you were in a room of fifty people and you looked us directly in the eyes to know if we were with you and we were, I think, almost all of us, and he said "I'll find you" and he did.

It had just started raining the night you came. Not a hard rain but enough to know the drought was over. Not hard like the very last night we met in Chile a year before the Coup and it was the *Dieciocho* and trouble beginning and when we stood in the downpour I said "*Nos vemos*" and you said "No. Not ever." And if you had said then "We have already had so much if we didn't see each other again it would be enough" you would have been right and wouldn't have been. It would not have been enough.

So don't flinch when I say it's not enough. I know it hurts you. I see it in your eyes. You look away wounded and lift your glasses the shield you wear against seeing. There's nothing wrong with your vision. The glasses are like safety goggles. Don't flinch when I say it's not enough or when I give you Charlie when you say "never." It's only that I'm pedaling.

It was five years ago when we were standing in the rain, and we have met since and will meet again. Then you hadn't known you'd have to leave the houses you've had to leave. I can't count the houses you've been in since, how many in Paris alone and how many in Amsterdam and how many in how many countries since that day you said we'd never meet again. You've spent New Year's Eve in a different country every year and this year you say it's the first time you're in a house where someone has lived longer than a year and you say this was a year of death and pain a terrible year the worst since 73. You can't close your eyes to it. But you have lived almost a year in one house and have another year to go in it and have two cats you hate but they live and require food and that is important. All of us need to remember that creatures live and require food and that we feed them. We all have death in our lives and we are scarred and we still live and we feed creatures, kids, and dogs and cats and friends and so we survive. We watch the ocean. You all have bicycles now in Amsterdam and can pedal like Antonio to the top of the mountain. Though your hearts may be broken, you pedal your bicycles to the mountain or

to the market against death and we keep our eyes
open all the time because we dare not shut them
because then we would not be safe but with our eyes
open we can see each other. That's the safety factor.

Do you remember we were walking on the beach
in the beginning in a soft rain and I met a man who
said he'd pray the sun up and you met a man who
said he'd find you and then despite the news reports
we saw a man with his feet pointing toward the
horizons wearing a black hat and carrying an
umbrella and the sea was full of fish and smelled like
the *sopa de mariscos* we ate in Chile and the man
said, "*Je suis Charlie Chaplin.*" Do you remember
what he said? He said, "*Je suis Charlie Chaplin.*"
And we listened to him. Seeing him with our own
eyes. Believing.

Where We Come From

The moment the soul is born, you feel it inside like a shadow, a weight which can not be measured. Suddenly, a light in the dark, a light so light it can not be seen, but a presence, nevertheless. It is a grave thing, this soul. It comes out of the grass where the dead sprawl. Everything under our feet was once born and died. The strength of the unborn rising in the constant smoke of green.

I am nothing without my dead. They are the conversation, the warning and the path. The soul is the one who speaks with them, who rises in her white hair, a mist of longing braids itself into the garland of whatever went before. Even the crystal has a soul if it remembers the ancestor stone; the wind, the fire, water, all have soul because they are attached to death.

Do not be afraid. An infinity of the dead stretch behind us holding us in their hands. We come out of their bodies. They whisper lullabies in our ears, and they hold us, forever, in their watery embrace.

Part the air, cut the water with a knife, comb the golden hair of the sun, find the dead waiting in the furrows. The living seed dropped into the soil wraps its roots about the dead and grows. It is the way. Every step forward falters without the backward glance.

Orpheus, the singer, had to look back. Were he to gain Eurydice and lose death, he would have had nothing. Her flesh dissolving, he stretched his hand back to her retreating shade and had her, and his life, forever.

That is one way.

What we push through is still there, bears the imprint of the slap of hands, the smear of transparent scent, is bent by the turn of a shoulder and the elongation of the thigh, receives the continual exhaust of bodies, carries our breath and all the other breaths.

The taste of you comes to me filtered through oranges and arguments, the silent howls of the invisible crowd the woman who is crying stands between us. Something is wet upon my cheek. Is it raining? Nothing can be thrown aside, but that the air passes the gesture on without comment.

How can I know who you are? Between us lie these exhalations, shouts, mutterings in sleep, all words dipped in saliva, spit out to be reabsorbed in each of our pores; we did not choose this coexistence.

Face to face, we spill what we have taken in, the air is humid, weighted with semantic moisture, breathing out breathing out, to empty ourselves of uninvited presences. But my chaste tongue is not innocent. I take in everything which has ever been uttered.

The air is carrier, witness, agent provocateur. Dare you whisper in your bed, I will receive the twitch of language through the still air which needs something to carry.

A Spiral in the Air

For Eloise Klein Healey and Pilgrim

It's not a proper name for something which flies the wind: a turkey vulture, looking for prey, swoops overhead. My friend speaks of China where the dragon and phoenix entwine as here the serpent and the eagle have been known to mate in the cylindrical air.

There is heat pulsing up from the earth. That dark geyser leaps up to the sun. Everywhere I look, the twining snakes rise into the cone of light.

It is not only in the heart, but in my back that I feel love, a knotty spine of caring, which I climb one step at a time, an impossible ladder, reaching from earthen feet toward the possibility of flight.

We climb it, while I, who am afraid of heights, watch the vulture and talk of China, other countries, where there are no rooms for everyone who wishes to make love and people marry late, while about my house the squirrels mate when their bodies are ready. There is no law or moral code instructing their tails to fold between their legs on tiny broken feet.

The turkey vulture finds the stairs, the ramps, the trembling foundations of wind and rises on the air. We see the determined beak as it dives almost to our eyes. There is a fire in its head feathers. Brazen, it arcs away, returns and glides away along a path I can not see.

Do you think there are no gods here? Everywhere, we are surrounded by the invisible, hearing more of what we can not hear than of the words we say. Then, when we do not speak, what joins us is under language, is the air under our tail feathers.

I sit in the afternoon with a poet friend. We speak of China, the dragon and the phoenix intertwining, while by my feet the rattler and the turkey vulture seek to mate.

We know this fire, but we do not speak of it. I'm no longer a girl. I do not say that this old fire has been rising in me toward an old fire bird in dark plumage who makes his nest in the air above my bed. What my friend knows, she also does not say.

And yet we know, we both have learned the movements, the spiral up the spine, the joining of the snake and bird, the double helix of heat. It takes so many years to master these. The phoenix and dragon are so old, old as China or the beginning of the world. And they still burn!

Lift us to you with your red beak.

It wasn't a dream, unless we shared it open-eyed, your car exploding into dream car, driving us further than we understood. Dreaming the road, we might dream only the first red stroke on a preliminary map, dream the cartographer, the engineer, and the man at the curve of the road with the sign, *Stop*.

It wasn't a dream, it wasn't the afternoon road, the trees light-speckled, it was bark and leaf, it was.... Moon stopped us, or wind, and a mud-stained pine root rose ghostly across our way. Stopped as in a dream, we stopped on the divided road and waited to build the road.

> I see,
> you see,
> the squirrel
> dragging her dead mate across the road.

There is the poem.

We do not dream this and we do not plunge into sorrow. Friendship is not prepared for what we see. We shift in the car from each other. This is a vision for lovers: the small creature, hobbled by her burden, teeth in the tail and claws too small to carry, insists her way across the road.

The two of them, the live one and the dead one, make their way to some leaf-mulched grave.

We stop and wait, then she—'he,' you say—skitters away, frightened by the shadows we cast, and we become pallbearers with twigs. "Do we dare?" you ask, and lay him—'her,' you say—under a tree. And then drive on.

It might have been a car that didn't stop, we say. What can friendship manage? Lovers might live the dream and build a temple at the sight of god in the afternoon dragging the lover back to the dark heart. But we did not dream this. The road was a road. We had to be cautious of our scent. Soon the ants would come.

I know this story and the irrevocable order of things.

The Death of the Wolf

For Pani Blue Hawk and Timber

I begin to dig the grave; the joy of the pickaxe against the stone, that splintering which only comes when metal strikes and what seems so solid is sheared.

She slept beside him all night. Her vigil now, as he had slept beside her, turning her to breathe. Those times when she was passing over to this side with equal struggle, crossing here from death, he found her, as she found him, under the tree, among the leaves. Their brokenness mended each other. The two serrated halves fit.

To glue one part to another, you must roughen the surface first. That which is smooth, or perfect, can not fit against another.

You bring the rain. Your dying breaks the clouds. The language of the sky drums upon the leaves and yellow blossoms of the acacia.

You are hovering about me. I can feel you in my nostrils, everywhere, every time I breathe.

The howl, both mournful and ecstatic, echoes. The death of the wolf, but not the death of the spirit.

There is a grief which has no earthly counterpart, though they say, here, this place, earth, is the only place death exists. This means, there is no life anywhere else. This means this place, this earth, is death's house.

It was something like a star going out or being born. That electric shudder, your entire body trembling, the current rushing also through my heart, your spirit shaking off the flesh. I can not believe it is the end of love. You always tended us so well.

"The spirit is gone," I said, "but he is still alive." And then, moments later, "He is dead."

In the afternoon, we knew a star had appeared somewhere in the universe. The great darkness punctured by a new light. I expect nothing less than such a flame from you, a sun which will burn ten billion years. Until we're all aflame or all put out.

A great beauty descended upon you in your death. The grace of your entire life coalescing into a moment of perfect sleep. I passed my hand over the yellow eyes which had become stones. In the morning, you moved, your belly rising with the first motions of the universe, the gases within you burning.

The other wolf stood at the edge and pushed the first dirt onto you with her nose. Now you are shaking the branches of the olive tree which will root about your bones. Your body, in the earth, on the knoll where we are permitted to bury only my ashes.

When I die, they will say, "She gave the wild a home. A wolf lived with her."

The olive leaf is dark on one side and full of light on the other.

The Bird in the Heart of the Tree

In honor of Reb Zalman Schacter

Seeing the movement down the tree, the descent of spirit into matter, or a singing bird, with blue feathers leaping from branch to branch.

How spirit breaks into song, how it must break itself into pieces to sing, how a part of that which is indivisible enters the universe in a body, a feather, a color or a note.

Spirit entering into form, breaks off from itself, breaks itself, breaks itself into pieces, is broken. Wherever we see spirit, there is something broken.

Here the heart is broken, here the spirit enters. The prayers of a broken heart call the spirit in, inevitably heal, are therefore whole.

The song enters the world. Here, there is someone singing. And a different melody, exactly the same, coming from farther away than time. The two songs meet in a corner of the garden. Perhaps in the very heart of the tree. *Tepheret* is the place of their meeting.

Or *Tepheret* is the place where the prayer is spoken. Or it is the place where the prayer is heard. Is the meeting place.

The bird is always praying. Even when it is asleep, the song is alive in it. The heart of the bird is a small drum, and the drum is beating out its song. When the dawn comes, the melody is awakened by the light. Or if it is a nightbird, it sings all night long.

To be the bird is lonelier than to be the song. The song is never lonely, but the bird is always longing for the song. In the moment of song, there is prayer, or in the moment of prayer there is song. Everything has a home.

Every prayer is answered. The bird in exile sending a message to the song or asking for the dawn to break. In the moment of prayer, exile disappears. When we feel that we have prayed well, it is because we've come home.

When I pray, I do not know whether I am climbing a tree or making a ladder for the light to climb down. Whether I am calling the bird to my hand or flying to meet it among the leaves.

But if I am the bird, what am I calling to myself? Is it a song? Or is it light? Or is it to be broken?

Sometimes the bird turns away. Sometimes it does not open its mouth to sing. Sometimes it is afraid. Sometimes it is afraid of the dark. But when it forgets it is afraid and opens its mouth to sing, it fills with light.

There was a place where we expected the birds to disappear. But because the heart was broken, the prayers existed nevertheless. No matter how heavy the earth, the air can always bear the song of birds.

The light of prayer travels faster than the speed of light. It takes no time for the light of prayer to travel between the worlds. So even in that place, prayer existed, and reached its destination. Even in that place. And even in that place, there are bird songs now.

Prayer can exit from any opening. And the light can enter us everywhere. The prayer is the call and the light is the answer. Or the bird calls and the song appears. They are like day and night. They are inseparable. Or indistinguishable.

As the light can enter anywhere, keep all the doors open for the singing.

Sometimes the birds sing so sweetly, the tree itself is made of light.

There is a hollow in the heart of a tree which was pecked out by the bill of a singing bird. Who knows the grief the tree felt with the incessant pecking. But now when you pass the tree, you can see that the hollow is full of light or rather it is full of song. And the bird? It is gone. It has work to do. Its work is pecking and singing.

In the moment of prayer, light shines on the invisible, and everything is seen.

To pray, to make oneself so willing, one is transparent, or empty enough for the song to enter.

Sometimes we are so busy praying, we do not hear the light calling out to us, looking for a place to rest.

Sometimes we are so busy praying, we can not see the singing, wanting to be heard.

The prayer and the response, the same: "I am here."

Sometimes gratitude, sometimes praise. Sometimes longing. A night owl on the one tree calling to another night owl in its branches.

A song without beginning and without end, breaking into notes, a light breaking into colors. All the pain of the breaking. And the beauty of it. The pain and the beauty. And that which is broken becomes whole. Prayer knows this.

Prayer is only the singing of one heart to another heart. And the beauty of it.

To get to it, to get to it, to get to it, prayer must travel so far in the dark to get to the light.

For the beauty of it. No prayer without beauty. And no beauty without prayer. And nothing without the heart of it. Beauty is the very heart of it. With all its brokenness, beauty is the heart of it.

In the Garden there is a Tree. And in the Tree is a Bird, a Bird with blue feathers. It sits in a nest it has carved into the very heart of the Tree. The Bird is singing. It is singing so sweetly, the Tree fills with Light. Perhaps the Song is the Light itself, perhaps the Light is the Song that the Bird with blue feathers has learned to sing.

A Song emerges from the Nest of Light in the Great Heart of the Tree. *Tepheret.* The Tree is full of Birds. Each Bird is full of Light. And the Light, it, is also Singing.

These Lights

I

A cracked cup which can not be mended and a bowl
with a tooth missing planted in the garden to catch
water, reflect the sky for the jays and robins, the
honeybees, who drink in the day and the frogs,
coyote and owl, after we are asleep, in the night.

When the sun rises across the fissure, there remains
the desire for night. Even in the daytime, the ones
who read the stars carry us across the night sky,
seeing behind the corona of sun toward the dark
curtain everywhere, that veil without end. It is only
here, or only on such small globes of meteoric dust
among the infinite expanses, that the daylight settles.
Its own corona, the gentle fire of pale blue, holds the
black at bay for a half turn.

In the dark sky, the wheels of the universe grind, the
light is gathered, cohered, fashioned into arrows
which descend into words. That rain. What comes
from beyond, comes only from the darkness. Or
across the darkness. Or through the darkness. Even
the light, especially the light, travels through the dark
in order to shatter in the blue plain. The dust of the
darkness adhering to its plumes of light.

To travel any distance beyond the voracity of the
Ouroboros, to escape from our own serpent mouth,
is to go into the dark. Start out in daylight if you
will, still, streaking up toward the ball of fire, you
will ultimately enter the dark. A light to guide you, a
series of beacons, a splatter of points of fire, yes,
those, but predominantly the dark holding them in its

omnipresent cradle, in the rocking shadows, a sky rhythm reflected in the seatide blood which is red and blue, fire and night.

A man speaking across the shapes which are constellated from light. And a woman. Voices gathering the light into shapes which also speak: The Dog in the sky; the Lion; Ursa; the Bear; the Arrow; the King; the Backbone of the Serpent; Al Kurhah, the Blaze in the Face of the Horse; Baculus Jacobi, Jacob's Rod; or Fiskikaller, the Staff; or Maria Rok and Mary's Distaff; or Siktut, the Seal-hunters.

Al Nitak, the Girdle, the Pleiades, the Sisters, the Starry Seven, Old Atlas' Children, or the General of the Celestial Armies, or the Flame, even the Razor, or Perv, Perven, Peren, all the Begetters. In China the women's stars, the Seven Sisters of Industry, as elsewhere Kimah, a Cluster or Heap, or as the Rabbis said, Sukkoth R'noth, the Tents of the Daughters. And beside them the belt from Al Mitakah, and Al Nathm, the String of Pearls, the Temple, the Wagon, the Shepherd of the Heavenly Flock. And Cygnus, the Swan, in full flight down the Milky Way, on gleaming wings, that Cross of Calvary, the Northern Cross, and nearby, Magdalen in Tears and Judas Iscariot, or earlier, Jacob, then Isaac with the Wood for the Sacrifice, or the Hebrew Sinner Gathering Sticks on the Sabbath, or Cain.

The universe in the sky descending into colors and density but no less itself, no less the Water-Beetle, the Wild Boar, the Wine cup of Noah, no less the Raven, the Red Bird, the Night Owl and the Bird of the Desert, no less Lupus, the Wolf, Zibu the Beast nor Urbat the Beast of Death nor the Star of the Dead Fathers, no less Benjamin nor the Wineskin, nor Bernice's Hair, for the starry points against the dark field over there, than the crow, here, streaking against the pale blue, caw, caw, or the Water Snake or the Wheat Field, the Harvest Keeper, there, than the water snake, here, another figure of light, the gold of the wheat field here in the bread, or the light and shadows of our hands bringing in the sheaves.

A bowl of water, or a mirror, something which catches and holds, what is above, what is below, and the man, or the woman, who steps across the curtains, gathering the day alongside the night, the blue face and the black, the light of form and the light of lights.

II

Nothing without the darkness. Everything within the darkness. The dark of the great globe, endlessly endless and contained, from which bolt all the luminous shapes raining down, and then settling, here, in the green or the dusty stones, in a hand, or a bowl of water. And these names, these bodies, these shapes, these images, as above so below, are the lights in the darkness and the light of the light in the great Tree.

The Tree of all the forests, ablaze, here and above, the invisible incandescent axis between the worlds, leaves of fire, or unconsuming flames on the bark, incalculable light years of burning.

And its roots, which could be and are rivers, underground streams, ley lines, force fields, are the divine waters, are also the flaming fissures in the molten rock which were once, and always remain, nothing but the light within, the interminable dark. The stars, here, no less than there. The black raven no more, no less, breathing than the waves of light breathing against the black feathers of the universe, and the bowl of water in the garden, after the rain, no less and no more, than the infinite broken chalice of night.

In the Morning   Walking

In Pueblo societies a kind of ultimate
democracy is practiced. Plants and animals are
also people and through certain rituals and dances
are given a place and voice in the political
discussions of the humans.... What we must find a
way to do, then, is incorporate the other people—
what the Sioux Indians called the creeping people
and the standing people and the flying people and
the swimming people—into the councils of
government."

Gary Snyder, from *Turtle Island*

In the morning, everyone is asleep. The woods
haven't awakened. Last night, I pushed the heart to
the breaking point, wanting the poem to explode
from the mad lady in a wild throw of cards and tea
leaves or shamanic visions, tearing the spiderwebs
from what is hidden wanting to know what is
coming and what has passed.

And this morning, it is quiet. Even the dreams asleep
in their walnut cradles and the evergreens pointing
delicate tips toward the mist. Last night, I looked for
fury and found it in a leaf where nothing is planned.
Last night, we talked till dawn, two bottles of wine,
whiskey, good dope, and now black coffee in a glass
under a tree. The bark peels off in ecstatic curls and
underneath a true human limb, extended, mahogany
and sensual entices me. I am shy of touching this
stranger, *madrone*, and wait for an invitation.

This morning, rain only from the top of the redwoods when the wind shakes us. The banana slug, companion to these trees in its insistent yellow walk, like kelp, like certain burls of trees, like unopened lilies, this slug, moving phallic wonder, extends across my path.

In the morning, the boy says, "the woods gives me everything," thinking of the desert where he was given only rocks, insupportable heat, also the curious lizard. Here there is water. And shade. And, if he has a gun, something alive to eat, a small fox or the bold deer which arrogantly stare into the loaded .22. Yet, there is also in the distance, the rooster reminding us of barns and boundaries, the domestic clock which insists on morning. The song I follow is the bird I can not see. And now my silence, so absolute, the hum of startled flies takes me by surprise.

This is the morning and my walk. I see only what the light falls on, though it's the dark I want to remember. The sun shines through, but what obstructs it, what it must bore through engages me. This dark, like Indians and dreams, rejects the camera, says, 'Nothing must be taken from the woods.'

This same morning, the boy says, "Let me walk in the woods with you," thinks I know the way. The way my poet friend asked me to take her to the beach. Walking is something I know about. I want to walk across the Sierra Nevada, the Sierra Madre, the Andes, walking toward the southern tip. Let's calculate—assume 10,000 miles at 20 miles a day, it's only a couple of years, 200 days to spare. Or if you want to walk with slugs, their pace is better, try 10 miles a day, it's simpler and still 95 days to spare—that is 3 months sitting in place like Indians unmoving and honoring the land—and 3 years walking. Just now I met a man who climbed the Andes for 6 weeks even without the language. It's only the pace that matters. If you weren't walking those 3 years what would you be doing?

Some mornings in these woods, I wake up talking, continue over eggs and orange juice and toasted muffins, securities from our common life. But sometimes, this morning, the woods call. Because there is no sun, nothing breaking through, only the wind, the slug, the jays, other rustlings in the undergrowth which do not ask permission. The woods teach us politics and co-existence. But we don't heed them. Whoever knows this secret, we put to death and then we bury them in crypts. So even the ghosts can not return, night or morning, to tell us, and no vegetables from our wisdom, this deprivation even of the compost fire.

In the mornings, I am always hearing unexpected voices. The woman who stopped me, asking, "Are you a gypsy or another of those dark skinned people, like Indians?" I was buying a silver hand against the evil eye for someone who had given me his protection. Amulets keep us safe but only when we do not escalate the evil. Nothing can keep us indefinitely from the useless shade we cast.

The difference between the tree and the umbrella: the first, even this morning, lets through some of the light and rain. We are too absolute about our territory. Death could be the democratic grist, promises a temporary resurrection in a knowable form. For example, my body, returning as a mushroom, nestling under a fern who is the man I love. We might be carrots together, squash. Life can be round as pumpkins. And death as bright. He and I running in long vines toward the sea. White flowers like morning glories become fruit. We're eaten—Thanksgiving—when you remember the Indians who tried to teach us this.

One morning, a conversation: I say, "There are only three good reasons for war. Food. Fertilizer. Religion." We don't even kill for god anymore, but for the hell of it. Hundreds of thousands. And since you won't eat my heart, then, at least let me astonish you, one morning, with my blossoms.

This morning, the woods, the mulch smell. Old sinking down, new pushing through. The old trees talking. A dead bird feeding some forest creatures, the common denominator of the species. The Indians are dead. Murdered. Yet fortunately, buried bare in the earth. Something still lurks in the trees, then, to give us warning.

At night, when you were in my body, when you were the tree giving breath to the night, I took it in. We lay there, your mouth open against mine with the breath going back and forth. I said, "This is the Amazon. I want to grow dark as a jungle with you, to feed all the myriad birds, to give off air to breathe." We lay together, dark woods feeding the universe, you breathing into me, I, taking your breath, holding it in my body, saying, "Life, Life, Life."

I wanted to be a plant form. I wanted to laugh under you like grass, to bend and ripple, to be the crisp smell, to be so common about you, to be everywhere about you, to house the small, and be there under your body when you rolled there, where I was.

I wanted to be the animal form. I wanted to howl, to speak the moon language, to rut with you as the August moon tipped toward roundness and the blood poured out of my body. I held your penis that had plunged into me, and afterwards my hands were red with my own blood. I wanted to paint our faces, to darken our mouths, to make the mark of blood across our bodies, to write "Life, Life, Life" in the goat smell of your hands. You carried it all day on your fingers, as I carried your pulse in my swollen cunt, the beat repeating itself like a heart. My body had shaped itself to yours, was opening and closing.

I wanted to be the forms of light, to be the wind, the vision, to burn you like a star, to wrap you in a storm, to make the tree yield. I wanted to drown in your white water, and where your fingers probed I wanted to hear each pore cry out, "Open, Open. Break Open! Let nothing be hidden or closed."

I wanted to be all the violences opening, all earthquake and avalanche, and the quiet, all the dawns and dusks, all the deep blues of my body, the closing and opening of light. I wanted to be the breath from the lungs of the universe, and to open your mouth with a tongue of rain, to touch all the corners and joinings. And when you entered me, when I heard you cry, "Love me, love me, love me with your mouth," I wanted to take you in with everything wet and fiery, to enter you with breath until you also called out and called out and called, "Life, Life, Life."

The leaves come down. The late yellow of winter, the color leached from the leaf. The leaves fall, the bougainvillaea is withered, the orange leaves curl from the frost. The towhee nests here this winter, instead of flying on. This transient visitor has become a resident. Mockingbirds also build their nests. The starlings have arrived, swallows, fly catchers, thrashers, finches, mourning doves, robins, sparrows, titmice, for this sanctuary of a bit of water in a broken bowl. I look for them in the morning, at dusk, and at night, listening for their warning songs. Their presence a warning presence, their beauty, ominous, in our neighborhood.

The weather has changed. The birds gather, come closer to the house. The shy quail fly into the garden, an eddy in the non-existent wind. A brown feather drops between the limbs of the trees. The dust rises a little and falls.

There is neither thunder nor lightning. If there is sound it is only the scratch of thistles, some small thirsty rodent dragging itself across a twig or the brittle sage leaning into the rock. A dry season without wisdom. The bark peels off the trunk, a sheaf of skin from a burned body. The rust smoke from the earth chimney spreads through the galaxy.

The task is to learn from the animals. And to learn from them is to provide for them, that is to preserve their territory, that is to withdraw, as the Ein Sof withdrew for the sake of creation.

To withdraw. To pull in one's horns. To lower the voice. To take up less room. To give the yard to the wolves. To offer the apricots to the birds. To put out water for the jay. To invite the deer. To stop on the road for the coyote to pass. To allow the snake its rock, to rejoice in the grizzly by the fence posts. To learn the names of the animals and the names of the stars.

This is what it has come to. This is the end of the poppies and the eucalyptus, the tulips and the golden fish. This is the end. A dull rust, an oak leaf bleached of its color, a sky gray and smudged. We had thought it would be different. We had thought we would die in a ruby blaze of fire or be preserved forever in the crystal glacial light passing over our feet. We had thought our death would be something glorious, the liquid of opals or the star sapphire alight in our eyes.

All day the ominous gray. The sky presses down upon us. There is weariness in heaven. A wind would bring rain, would stir up the salt water, would make the ocean dance, but nothing stirs under the gray fatigue except the birds.

But now it is late afternoon. Now they come again with their flickering shades of bronze and green, with their flashes of blue and yellow, with their asides of red and black. A fire in the garden on the wet wings of birds. A maelstrom of color. A waterfall of brown, orange and white. It would be ignoble all of it, mean and ignoble, if the garden weren't full of birds, their feathers, lemon and amber lights, under the still green leaves, these last flowers of the eucalyptus and the oak.

Star Walk

Walking at night under the remaining stars. Something lethal stirring the scent of dry sage and early narcissus. Something slightly chemical chafing the odor of the turned earth and the snorting horses. The night wind slithers through the gully, cold and sharp, a momentary freshening.

Outside the rare realm of leaves and bare earth, thoughts both metallic and mechanical rasp through the mind like a chain saw, cutting small pieces into smaller pieces. The dreams disappear, not even as fallen leaves, but as leaves which have failed to sprout, like the yolk of the poisoned egg which will never be a bird. The disappearance of the unborn. What might have been. Unbearable.

Danger everywhere, signs and portents, miracles and catastrophes. The hammer of one ambition against another, fusion and fission. And then an unending firestorm in the mind. Enter the grim reaper of the death of spirit. Alarmed, I put my hand into the poultice of earth.

At my feet, a wild trapezoid of new grace, her legs angling away from her body in a stretch of memory holding snow, the midnight sun, the blue continuous night in her paws, and despite that radiance, Isis, the great white wolf of the Arctic, is helpless against the disappearance of the time before, the time before, the time before; endless time disappearing.

To walk into the unknown to make it known may not be the way. To open the door underground and pass through flooding it with Herculean light, may not be the way. To streak in a straight line into the sky, trail of gases blazing, may not be the way. Traveling forward in a straight line to the end of the universe without looking back, afraid even of the opalescent curve at the end of the shell of time, may not be the way.

Where is the smaller circle which cycles ends and beginnings? Small is the ring finger, is the curve of a belly, is the rotation of the earth, is the spin of spring out of winter. A walker along the earthy meridians catches the seasons and the repetitions of day and night.

Not to break open the egg. Not to split anything apart. Not to divide what does not wish to be sundered. Not to release what wishes to be hidden. No great flashes of light and heat. No machinations of the dark. Not to transform what wishes to persist. Not to make light from stones. Light to light, matter to matter. Let the clear water remain itself.

To come back. To begin again. To repeat ourselves. To start again. To flourish, die and sprout.

A marriage. The same man. The same woman. Companions from one generation to another. The same table. The same plates. The same soup. Onion, garlic, celery, pepper and carrots. A bay leaf. Oregano and basil. A silver ladle from the ancestors.

The familiar and welcome bread. Salt and honey. The same bed. The thinning sheets washed, dried, washed, thrashed, washed. Again. The Sabbath. And again. The begetting and the begat. Something modest and recurrent. Green.

Walking at night. The first hoot of the owl. And the answer. The great shadow within the emptiness of the bough of a tree. The return of the great birds to a nest of air, to the wind warming itself in the chatter of leaves. We walk within the circle of the moon, the wintergreen light burning into our eyes.

Along the same road, along the same hills, rising and falling. You take my hand again. I close my eyes and open them. Everything stays the same. We walk on. The neighbor's dog barks again and darts between our legs, again. I trip again. You steady me again. Trace of orange blossoms, tincture of eucalyptus.

The older Timber wolf inclines toward the beckoning of the grave beneath the olive tree. When the sun dies, it is born again. The hag of the moon returns as a slip of a girl. Welcome night wind. Let this small breath of air remain. Leave it for the owl hoot, for the whistle of night birds, for the singing of frogs spiraling toward the pole of the North star in the steady circle of the Dipper and Cassiopeia.

War at the horizon. Fear when the sun sets that a fire will remain in the morning sky. That what is rosy in the sky is the other light which comes only out of our darkness.

If there is a storm and you can not escape it, you go to the eye, to the very heart, and move with it. At least you will survive. At least you.

In the moment of diving into the heart of the storm for protection, I am the storm. Who else is at the heart of the fire storm but myself?

When the stars appear, it is not eternity but their constancy which reassures the heart of the nature of the universe. The stars appearing on the great tree of light which burns and is not consumed, shine down.

A dismembered cat howling in the wilderness of the coyote's mouth awakened us in the dawn to the ubiquity of pain. Shrieks like the rain which does not come.

Whatever storm is imminent, it will be a fire storm, unless we wait more patiently and longer than we can bear for what we remember is rain. Trees, hungry for water, struck by lightning, blaze in protest, but blaze nevertheless.

The other rain will come to them if not to us, in the time which extends itself beyond time. We have put ourselves against the rain.

We have put ourselves against the mountain. We have put ourselves against the sea. Cuchulain the maddened god tied himself to a tree and fought with the sea for three days after he had blindly killed his son. The tree held him fast so he could spend his grief. We have put ourselves against the tree.

The two white Sabbath candles must be lit exactly at sunset but the firebraid at the end of the Sabbath need never be lit. But then the Sabbath continues forever unless the single intricate braid and the four wicks first blaze and are extinguished in the crucible of red wine.

The sun has set and still we have not lit the first candles. Are we too late for a Sabbath?

It is afternoon and we are lighting the two white candles late because we are afraid of the Sabbath, of the Peace Which Passeth Understanding. And afraid, we are too late.

It is so simple to understand. Who is killed in a war? The sons and daughters are killed in a war. It is so easy to understand.

The tree will not be able to bear the weight of the grief which is coming. And the water will not be able to engulf the salt of our tears. And the mountain will not bury us within its heart. And the rain? Let us not ask mercy from the rain.

Therefore be vigilant to discover the exact instant of the setting of the sun. At the green flash, strike the match so that the light is not extinguished and the Sabbath becomes one with the rosy mantle of the sky.

Learn to bear Peace though it will sear your heart. For the stillness will come like a storm which has no eye and from which there is no escape. And you will burn like the tree which has been struck by lightning and offers itself up and is not consumed. Or like the rain of stars which burn and also are not consumed.

And afterwards there will be no darkness such as you have always known.

Heart Break

For Victor Turner,
then for Barbara Myerhoff.

When a great heart breaks,
as it must,
we gather the pieces
into ourselves
and are made whole
thereby.

Peace is coming
in a great wave,
this green wind,
the earth,
     is breathing.

Prayer

I want
to get to the heart
of it

 and every living thing

for God
is there.

Parallax Press publishes books on Buddhism, mindful awareness, and social responsibility, including the following poetry books:

Temple Dusk: Zen Haiku, by Mitsu Suzuki

Looking for the Faces of God, by Deena Metzger

True Body, by Miriam Sagan

Yellow Dog Journal, by Judith Minty

Without Warning, by Patricia Donegan

All Possible Surprises, by Gene Knudsen-Hoffman

For a free catalog of these titles as well as our other books and tapes, please write to:

Parallax Press
P.O. Box 7355
Berkeley, CA 94707